GOLF LEGENDS
of All Time

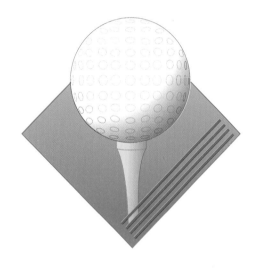

Al Barkow

David Barrett

Publications International, Ltd.

Al Barkow is the editor-at-large of *Golf Illustrated* and the former editor-in-chief of *Golf Illustrated* and *Golf*. He has been a freelance writer for sports magazines, including *Sports Illustrated*, *Golf Digest*, and *Golf Journal*. He is the author of *Golf's Golden Grind: The History of the Tour* and *Gettin' to the Dance Floor: An Oral History of American Golf*. He was a contributing writer to *20th Century Golf Chronicle*.

David Barrett is a senior editor at *Golf*. He was a contributing writer to *20th Century Golf Chronicle*, *The Wit & Wisdom of Golf, Golf in America: The First One Hundred Years,* and *The PGA Championship: 1916 – 1984*.

Editorial Assistants: Candice Cummins Sunseri, Mark Gearen

Contents

CONTENTS

Introduction

A field of elite golfers appeared in the 1940 Goodall Round-Robin. Pictured are (front row, left to right) Ben Hogan, Byron Nelson, Jimmy Demaret, Dick Metz, Craig Wood, Paul Runyan, and Clayton Heafner. Also posing are (back row, left to right) Henry Picard, Martin Pose, Jimmy Hines, Horton Smith, Gene Sarazen, Lawson Little, Jimmy Thompson, and Sam Snead.

*B*en Hogan, 16 months removed from a horrific auto accident that ravaged his body, was now on the verge of winning the 1950 U.S. Open. He led by three strokes with seven holes to play. However, his still-damaged legs throbbed in pain, and after his tee shot at the 12th hole, he nearly fell.

Hogan hobbled toward Harry Radix, a friend nearby. "Let me hang onto you, Harry," Ben said. "My God, I don't think I can finish."

Hogan limped through the next six holes, and by the 18th tee he had fallen back into a tie. Somehow, he needed to muster a heroic approach shot to keep his hopes alive. . .and he did just that. Stroking a 1-iron, Hogan launched a majestic shot that settled safely on the green. In agony, he two-putted for a tie. The next day, he prevailed in an 18-hole playoff.

It was the stuff legends are made of.

It is also one of the many captivating stories you'll find in *Golf Legends of All Time,* a book that honors the 70 greatest golfers who ever picked up a club. *Golf Legends of All Time* focuses mostly on PGA Tour greats, but the whole spectrum of golfdom is covered: LPGA stars, foreign golfers, course designers, and oft-forgotten pioneers. The roots of golf dig so wide and deep that even Scotland's Old Tom Morris, who whacked a featherie ball in the 1840s, earned a place in these pages.

The biographies in *Golf Legends of All Time* are all-encompassing, chronicling the golfers' lives from their early years through the lengths of their careers. Yet the profiles go well beyond the facts. The biographies explore the golfers' personalities, recount their fascinating personal stories, and relive their greatest golfing heroics.

The personalities of the 70 legends run the gamut, from the terse and demure to the chatty and jolly. Prior to tournament golf, Babe Zaharias performed on vaudeville, tap-dancing and playing the harmonica. Walter Hagen, though, was golf's ultimate showman. So brazen was "Sir Walter" that he sometimes sent his caddie 150 yards ahead to pull the flagstick. Then there was Bobby Locke. The stately South African so annoyed American players in the 1940s that they called him "Muffin Face." The jowly Locke dressed in knickers, a white cap, and white shoes and strolled deliberately down the golf course as he pontificated about his next stroke. When a reporter would ask him a question that was instructional in nature, Locke boldly requested $100 for his response.

Somewhere in the lives of these golfers lie compelling personal stories—sometimes comic, sometimes tragic. Lee Trevino grew up in a house with no electricity or running water, yet he was able to scrape together needed money through his golf skills and wild imagination. Trevino hustled golfers with a Dr Pepper bottle, hitting shots with the fat end and pool-cueing putts with the thin end. Young Tom Morris remains golf's saddest story. Old Tom's son won four British Opens by age 21, but he died three years later. Morris never recovered from the shocking death of his wife and baby, who both died during childbirth.

When it comes to heroic golf shots, few could match the wallop of Gene Sarazen at the 1935 Masters. Down three strokes to Craig Wood with four holes to play, Sarazen erased the entire deficit with one swing of a 4-wood, as his second shot on the par-5, 485-yard 15th rocketed to the green and then glided softly into the cup. Sarazen won in a playoff the next day. As for famous hot streaks, Byron Nelson blazed the trail with his 11 straight victories in 1945. His streak included the spectacular—he won the Iron Lung Open with a Tour-record 263 total—as well as the dramatic—he birdied five of the last six holes to win the Philadelphia Inquirer Invitational by one stroke.

If you want to learn about Seve Ballesteros's miracle shot from the parking lot, or Sammy Snead's sourpuss uncle, then spend some time with *Golf Legends of All Time*. Every star has a story to tell.

Babe Zaharias hugs her clubs during the 1947 British Ladies' Open Amateur. That year, she became the first American to win the event—one of the many "firsts" for the great Zaharias.

Willie Anderson

Anderson's swing mechanics were a mess, yet he displayed uncanny accuracy with his mashie and driver. Moreover, the stoic Anderson rarely cracked under pressure.

It is difficult to assess Willie Anderson's stature among the greats of the game. He competed when golf was in its infancy in America, with relatively primitive equipment and course conditioning, so it's pointless to compare scores. But one thing is certain: He was the first dominant player in American golf.

There were only two significant tournaments in the United States when Anderson played at the turn of the century, the U.S. Open and Western Open, and he won each event four times. His total of four U.S. Open titles has been matched only by Bobby Jones, Ben Hogan, and Jack Nicklaus, and not surpassed. Anderson is the only player ever to have won three straight Opens, claiming the title from 1903–05. His 73 in 1903 and 72 in 1904 established 18-hole Open records. He finished in the top five in 11 Opens, a record that only Nicklaus has tied.

Anderson emigrated to the U.S. at the age of 17 along with his father, who was a greenkeeper in North Berwick, Scotland. Willie took a club job in Rhode Island, the first of 10 clubs he would work for in his 14 years in America.

The slightly built Anderson was an accurate player, but his strength on the course was considered to be his calm demeanor. This served him well in 1901 when he won his first Open at Myopia Hunt Club in Massachusetts. He trailed by five strokes with five holes remaining in a playoff against Alex Smith before finishing with five straight 4s to win by one.

Anderson finished fifth in the Open in 1902, but the next year at Baltusrol's original course in New Jersey, he claimed his second title, again in a playoff. He won the 1904 Open at Glen View outside Chicago by shooting his record 72 in the final round, then nipped Alex Smith again at Myopia in 1905. Anderson played in five more Opens but never again finished better than fourth. His death in 1910 came suddenly; he played three 36-hole matches the week before.

Anderson's three straight U.S. Open triumphs is a feat that's never been equaled. He also seemed to challenge the record for most club jobs, as he worked for 10 different American clubs including Baltusrol, where he won his second Open.

Tommy Armour

Above: *Armour clutches the U.S. Open Trophy after defeating Harry Cooper in an 18-hole playoff at Oakmont C.C. in 1927. Opposite page: Armour struggled at times with his putter but was deadly accurate with his fairway woods and irons.*

Had the Masters started before he turned 39, Tommy Armour might have achieved the modern Grand Slam of winning all four professional major events. As it was, the man known as the "Silver Scot" settled for victories in the U.S. Open, PGA Championship, and British Open, all of them in dramatic fashion.

Armour was born in Edinburgh, Scotland, in 1895 and lost sight in an eye while fighting in World War I. He emigrated to the United States after coming over to play in the Walker Cup Matches in 1922, and he turned pro in 1924. His timing was good—the pro tour was just then developing, with most of the events taking place in the winter when the pros could get away from their club jobs.

Armour's first big victory came in the 1927 U.S. Open at Oakmont thanks to a heroic finish. He played the last six holes in 2-under-par, and he birdied the 72nd hole by hitting a 3-iron to within 10 feet of the hole to tie Harry Cooper. The magnificent stroke helped earn Armour a reputation as one of the finest iron players in the game. He won the 18-hole playoff by coming from two strokes down with six holes to play.

In the 1930 PGA Championship, Armour defeated Gene Sarazen, one of the top players of the day, in the 36-hole final match when he holed a 12-foot putt for par on the last hole and Sarazen missed from 10 feet. But the title that meant the most to Armour came the next year when he won the British Open at Carnoustie in his native Scotland. He trailed by five strokes entering the final round, but he stormed home with a 71 for a winning 296 total.

Shortly thereafter, Armour began to have trouble holing short putts and invented the term "the yips" to describe his affliction. He ended his career with 24 professional victories. In his later years, Armour became one of the most well-known—and high-priced—golf teachers in America. His book *How to Play Your Best Golf All the Time* is considered an instruction classic.

GOLF LEGENDS OF ALL TIME

John Ball

*I*f not for the incomparable Bobby Jones, England's John Ball would be considered the greatest amateur golfer of all time. In a career spanning the 19th and 20th centuries, Ball racked up eight victories in the British Amateur, the most titles by any player in a single major championship. The first of those titles came in 1888 and the last in 1912, mirroring Jack Nicklaus's modern feat of winning major championships over a 24-year span.

It is difficult to compare Ball's record with the records of those who came later, or even with contemporaries Harry Vardon, John H. Taylor, and James Braid, who ruled the professional game during the same period. But esteemed golf writer Bernard Darwin, who saw all the greats of the first part of the 20th century, wrote, "I have derived greater aesthetic and emotional pleasure from watching John Ball than from any other spectacle in any other game."

Ball enjoyed one great moment against the professionals. He won the 1890 British Open at Prestwick in Scotland, becoming the first Englishman to claim that title. He also won the British Amateur that year; he and Jones are the only two players to sweep those titles in the same year. Ball nearly repeated the feat in 1892 when he finished second in the British Open.

Ball was born in 1861 in Hoylake, England, where his father owned the Royal Hotel. The hotel was near the Royal Liverpool Golf Club, where Ball learned the game. In the first British Amateur in 1885, held at Royal Liverpool, Ball beat his father, 4 & 2, in the third round before losing in the semifinals.

Ball's first British Amateur title came at Prestwick in 1888. His other titles followed in 1890, '92, '94, '99, 1907, '10, and '12. In the 1899 final, Ball came from five down to beat Freddie Tait in 37 holes. Ball missed three years of competition (he served in the Boer War) before coming back to claim his last three titles. He played his last British Amateur in 1921, at the age of 60, making it to the fifth round.

Opposite page: Ball, at age 61, is pictured with his caddie at Hoylake, England, where Ball was born and learned to play golf. Left: By the time he was 17, in 1878, Ball had finished fourth in the British Open. His eight British Amateur titles are an all-time record for victories in a major championship, amateur or professional, men's or women's.

Seve Ballesteros

Seve Ballesteros dashed onto the golf scene with all the flair of the great matadors of his native Spain. Like the bullfighters, Ballesteros often flirted with danger.

Those who witnessed it will never forget the 1979 British Open at England's Royal Lytham and St. Annes. The 22-year-old Ballesteros, tall and slender, darkly handsome, was swinging his driver with reckless abandon, and the ball was responding accordingly, flying every which way but straight. With his driver, he would hit only eight fairways through the four rounds. One was not expected to win any championship with such wildness off the tee, but especially not at Royal Lytham, notorious for its narrow, oddly angled fairways and severe rough. But Ballesteros's counter was an extraordinary talent for recovery around the greens; he was a brilliant pitcher, chipper, sand bunker player, and putter from in close.

At the start of the last round, Ballesteros was two strokes behind Hale Irwin and only one ahead of Jack Nicklaus, both far more conservative players and far more experienced in championship play. Ballesteros took no heed, and he took the lead after the 2nd hole with a birdie and a par. At the 6th, he hooked his drive a full 90 yards off-line, into the 14th fairway. His second shot went 50 yards through the green. He got his par. Continuing to play more often than not from the rough, he held his lead going into the back nine. It was at the 16th, though, where his reputation was made for all time. On the 353-yard par-4, Ballesteros drove 30 yards off-line to the right and into a parking area for television production vans. From there, he wedged to within 14 feet of the hole and made the putt that in short time ensured his victory. He was dubbed "The Car Park Champion."

Above: *In a brilliant run from 1979–84, Ballesteros won more than 20 tournaments worldwide, including two Masters and two British Opens. Opposite page: The flamboyant, emotional Seve became one of the most popular players on both sides of the Atlantic.*

GOLF LEGENDS OF ALL TIME

Ballesteros put his resourcefulness on display in the final round of the 1991 Ryder Cup when he blasted out of this predicament on No. 2 at Kiawah Island to win the hole from American Wayne Levi.

Seve Ballesteros was born in 1957 in Pedrena, a small town in rural northern Spain. His father was a farm laborer who worked in fields near the golf course where Seve caddied and learned to play. He began to play early, at around age seven, following the lead of his older brother, Manuel, who would also become a golf professional. To say Ballesteros played golf in those earliest years is not quite the word. He had come into possession of a 3-iron, the only club he would own for a year or so. And, of course, the young farm worker's boy was certainly not allowed to play on the only course within many miles, a private club. He would in time, when his talent would be recognized.

Until then, these deprivations would turn out to be of great benefit. Seve would play every imaginable shot with that 3-iron—low ones, high ones, draws, fades, hooks, and slices, hitting the ball out of deep grass in a farm field, off hard dirt roads, out of sand. He often played his shots to tomato cans he sunk into the ground at the back of his modest home. Ballesteros would acknowledge years later that the versatility of his game, with all clubs, was born in those days with his lone 3-iron as his companion.

Because of his humble origins, a higher education was not in the cards for Ballesteros. His skill at golf was apparent while he was in his teens, and at the age of 17 he turned professional. A scant two years later, having gained some experience playing the European Tour—and winning once—Ballesteros finished in a tie for second with Nicklaus in the 1976 British Open won by Johnny Miller. It was a stunning achievement for someone with so little seasoning at that level of competitive golf.

Seve liked the taste of it, and with what everyone came to know as soaring self-confidence, Ballesteros became a major factor on the European circuit and finally worldwide. From 1976–78, he won 11 tournaments—10 in Europe and one in the United States (the 1978 Greensboro Open). Thus, in winning the 1979 British Open, he didn't in fact become a star overnight. It just seemed that way, because for the first time he was on a major stage, playing in the oldest championship in golf, and on international television.

Through 1996, Ballesteros had won at least 60 tournaments around the world, including three British Opens. Nine of those victories came on the U.S. PGA Tour, two of them in the Masters. He was also a potent figure in the revival of interest in the Ryder Cup Matches. Seve played on the European team seven times from 1979–95. And while with his play he won more than enough points for his side, it was as much his spirited, even emotional ardor for the competition that spurred the success of his teams.

Ballesteros receives the coveted green jacket from defending Masters champion Craig Stadler after winning at Augusta in 1983. Seve finished at 280 to win by four strokes over Tom Kite and Ben Crenshaw.

Jim Barnes

Standing 6′3″, Long Jim Barnes towered over most of the golfers of his day. He also was one of the best players in the game in the period just before and after World War I, winning all of what were then considered major championships (the U.S., British, and Western Opens and the PGA Championship).

Barnes was born in 1887 in Cornwall, England, where he became an assistant professional at age 15. He emigrated to America four years later, though he retained his English citizenship. Barnes was a quiet and gentlemanly man who let his golf clubs do the talking and often walked the course with blades of grass clenched in his teeth.

Barnes's greatest performance came in the 1921 U.S. Open at Columbia Country Club in Chevy Chase, Maryland. He led by three strokes after the opening day and extended his margin after each round to four, seven, and then nine strokes at the finish—the biggest victory margin this century. He was serenaded up the 18th fairway by a Marine band and is the only Open champion ever to receive the trophy from the president, with Warren Harding doing the honors.

Barnes also has the distinction of winning the first two PGA Championships ever held, in 1916 and then in 1919 after a two-year gap due to World War I. He edged Jock Hutchison in the first one when he holed a five-foot putt on the 36th hole and Hutchison missed from the same distance to give Barnes a 1-up win. Barnes whipped Fred McLeod, 6 & 5, in 1919.

Although the pro tour consisted of only a few scattered events each year in Barnes's day, he is credited with 20 wins in the U.S. These include the 1914, '17, and '19 Western Opens. He capped his career by winning the 1925 British Open, considered somewhat of a surprise since he had not played particularly well in the previous couple of years. He came from five strokes back to win, taking advantage of Macdonald Smith's collapse in the final round at Prestwick.

Opposite page: In 1925, Barnes followed a victory in the British Open with a 12 & 11 rout of Willie Macfarlane for the unofficial world championship at Columbia C.C. near Washington, D.C. Below: "Long Jim" coils for a putt. At 6′3″, he towered over most of his rivals.

GOLF LEGENDS OF ALL TIME

Patty Berg

She came from a most unlikely region of the United States to become a great golfer, but that was the way of Minnesotan Patricia Jane "Patty" Berg. She was not daunted by any obstacles thrown in her way.

Born in 1918, Berg began her athletic career as a speed skater, competing in national events. When she was 13, she began swinging a golf club in her backyard. Noting her interest in this game, Berg's father, a member of the Interlachen C.C. (where Bobby Jones won one of his Grand Slam victories, the 1930 U.S. Open), sent his youngest daughter for instruction with the club pro. Not long after, she started taking lessons from Lester Bolstad, the University of Minnesota golf coach who would work with Berg for the next 40 years. At 15, Berg entered the Minneapolis City Ladies championship and shot a 122 in the qualifying round. The next year in the same event, she won the qualifying medal and the tournament.

With that, her father began entering Patty in important national amateur tournaments and taking the family to Florida for at least a month every winter. In 1935, Patty reached the finals of the U.S. Women's Amateur championship. She would win that title in 1938, and in all would capture 28 amateur championships over a period of seven years. She played on two U.S. Curtis Cup teams, in 1936 and 1938.

In 1939, on her way to defending one of her amateur titles, Berg met with the first of a number of serious physical problems. She had an emergency appendectomy that hospitalized her for a month and essentially ended her competitive season. In 1941, while

Below: Berg, age 18, checks her mechanics in preparation for Curtis Cup competition in 1936. Opposite page: Berg (center) receives the first-place trophy from Augusta, Georgia, mayor Dick Allen after winning the first of three consecutive Titleholders championships in 1937.

driving from Texas to Tennessee to play an exhibition to raise funds for British War Relief, the car in which she was driving with fellow pro Helen Dettweiler was hit. Berg's left knee was broken in three places, and she ended up with 75 percent use of the leg in terms of bending it. After taking therapy with a prizefighter named Tommy Littleton, she returned to the golfing wars.

Berg turned professional in 1940. She wasn't the first woman golf pro, but she was among the first 10. At the time, women professionals usually

Right: Berg's hardware included this trophy for winning the 1938 U.S. Women's Amateur, when she defeated Estelle Lawson Page in the final, 6 & 5. Below: A powerful, accurate driver, Berg won 57 professional tournaments despite a series of debilitating injuries.

did not give lessons and were relegated to administrative jobs. What's more, there were very few tournaments for women pros. When Berg became a pro, there were only a handful of tournaments in which she could play, with total purse money around $500. But in the face of such a dismal situation, Berg persisted. She earned most of her income giving exhibitions and clinics for the Wilson Sporting Goods Company, with whom she signed a contract upon turning pro. In her lifetime, the short, stocky Berg would give some 10,000 clinics all over the country, all of them with characteristic high spirits and enthusiasm. She was one of women's golf's most energetic and effective ambassadors.

Patty also did something about the competitive circumstances for women pros. After serving in the Marine Corps during World War II (Lieutenant Berg worked as a recruitment officer), she embarked on creating a pro tournament circuit for women on which she would become one of its early stars. Berg

was instrumental in reorganizing the Women's Professional Golf Association. "Women's" was changed to "Ladies" (LPGA), Fred Corcoran was hired to book events and promote them, and the Wilson Company was prompted to put up administrative costs for the first six years. Berg was the LPGA's first president. With the foundation of the circuit set, Berg went out and played.

Berg is pictured in 1959, the year she became the first woman to record a hole-in-one in USGA competition and eight years after her induction into the LPGA Hall of Fame.

Berg had won six times before the LPGA was formed, and from 1948–62 she captured 44 more titles with a game that featured brilliant shot-making with fairway woods and outstanding putting. Her victories included the first U.S. Women's Open, in 1946, which was then played at match play; six Western Opens; and four Titleholders Championships. Her last professional victory came in the Muskogee Civitan Open in 1962, when she was 44 years old.

Berg was forced by a hip replacement to end her professional playing career in 1980, but as always she continued giving exhibitions and clinics with her usual zest until she was well into her 70s—and that despite cancer surgery in 1971, major hip surgery in 1980, and back surgery in 1989. Nothing, it seemed, could keep Patty Berg down.

Of course, Berg had numerous awards to honor her long work in and for golf. She was inducted into at least 10 Halls of Fame. She was one of the first four inductees to the LPGA's Hall and one of the first two women inducted into the PGA/World Golf Hall of Fame. She also won the 1963 Bob Jones Award, one of the USGA's highest honors. And just to remind everyone that she was as much a player as a teacher and promoter of golf, in 1991, at the age of 73, she made a hole-in-one.

Julius Boros

*H*is easygoing manner was matched by a casually elegant swing. But while Julius Boros came to the golf course with the air of a man heading to his local fishing hole to spend a relaxing day, he was at his best in the game's biggest events, particularly the U.S. Open. Boros won the Open twice, in 1952 and 1963, and his 11 top-10 finishes in the event trail only Jack Nicklaus, Ben Hogan, and Arnold Palmer since World War II.

Boros was an accountant in Connecticut until he turned pro in 1950 at the age of 30. Despite the late start, he went on to have a long career, sustaining a high standard of play into his late 40s and even his 50s. He is the oldest man to have won a major title, capturing the 1968 PGA Championship at age 48. He ranked among the top five money winners at 47 and 48. And in 1975, at age 55, he lost the Westchester Classic in a sudden-death playoff.

Boros's first of 18 PGA Tour victories came in the 1952 U.S. Open at the Northwood Club in Dallas, where he posted a 68 in the third round and won by four strokes. Boros also won the World Championship of Golf in 1952 and again in 1955, leading the money list in those years.

Boros had his ups and downs over the next several years, but he hit a high note at the 1963 U.S. Open. He birdied two of the final three holes of regulation to reach a playoff at The Country Club in Brookline, Massachusetts, then fired a 70 to beat Arnold Palmer and Jacky Cupit. Boros also beat out Palmer in the 1968 PGA Championship, shooting a closing 69 to win by one stroke.

Though the Senior Tour came along a little late for Boros, he played a role in getting it off the ground. He teamed with Roberto De Vicenzo to beat Tommy Bolt and Art Wall in a six-hole playoff at the 1979 Legends of Golf, an event generally credited with spawning the Senior Tour the next year.

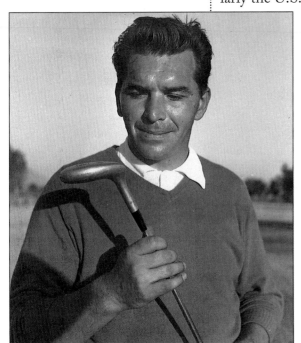

Above: Boros admires his putter after firing a 66 in the first round of the 1952 Phoenix Open. Opposite page: Boros (right) survived a three-way playoff to capture the 1963 U.S. Open at The Country Club. Alongside is Francis Ouimet, who won the Open on the same course 50 years before.

Bradley more than offset the agony of an occasional missed putt with remarkable consistency. In her first 22 years on the LPGA Tour, she posted 206 top-five finishes and became the first player in LPGA history to pass $2, $3, and $4 million in career earnings.

GOLF LEGENDS OF ALL TIME

Pat Bradley

She has been one of the most consistent LPGA players over the last couple of decades on the LPGA Tour, but Pat Bradley made her biggest impact on the game with one glorious year. In 1986, she won three of the LPGA's four major championships: the Nabisco Dinah Shore, LPGA Championship, and du Maurier Classic, failing to capture only the U.S. Women's Open. The only two other LPGA players to win three majors in a year were Babe Zaharias in 1950 and Mickey Wright in 1961. Bradley has claimed six majors in all and is the only player to have won all four of the "modern" LPGA majors, having claimed the U.S. Women's Open in 1981 (she also won the du Maurier in 1980 and '85).

Bradley grew up in Westford, Massachusetts, where she was an avid skier, but she worked hard on her golf game at Florida International University and joined the LPGA Tour in 1974. Her first win came two years later. The high point of the first decade of her career came in the 1981 U.S. Women's Open when she shot a final-round 66 to outduel Beth Daniel and win by one stroke.

Until 1986, it appeared that Bradley was destined to be known more for coming close than for winning. She entered that year with 16 wins, but 35 runner-up finishes. She had finished in the top four on the money list six times, but never in first place. Nor had she ever won the Player of the Year Award or the Vare Trophy for low scoring average. Bradley swept those awards in 1986 when she had five wins and six seconds, then repeated the feat in 1991 when she won four times.

An accurate iron player, Bradley annually ranks among the LPGA leaders in fairways hit and greens in regulation. She played an LPGA-record 61 subpar rounds in 1991 and boasts six career holes-in-one.

Bradley's career took a downturn in 1988 when she was diagnosed with hyperthyroidism. But, after taking time off to treat the condition, one of the game's most intense competitors came back determined to reach 30 wins and qualify for the LPGA Hall of Fame. She accomplished her goal by winning eight times from 1989–91. Bradley added a 31st win in 1995 and has more than $5 million in career earnings.

James Braid

*B*y the turn of the 20th century, golf had expanded well beyond the borders of its Scottish birthplace and was catching on rapidly in England and the United States. Indeed, two of the Great Triumvirate who dominated the British Open in the 20 years before World War I, Harry Vardon and John H. Taylor, were Englishmen. The third, James Braid, was a Scot, the son of a humble Elie plowman. But even Braid went to England to embark on his golf career, heading to London to become an apprentice clubmaker in 1893 at the age of 23.

A tall man, Braid was a long hitter for his day. Early golf historian Horace Hutchinson wrote that Braid swung with "a divine fury." Nonetheless, it took him a while to harness his considerable skills, and he was the last of the Great Triumvirate to win a British Open. Braid played in his first Open in 1894. In 1895, he began to make a name for himself by halving a match with Taylor, the 1894 and '95 Open champion.

Braid finished second in the Open in 1897, then in 1899 finished fifth to begin an incredible streak. For 14 straight Opens, Braid was never out of the top five, a feat that has never been matched (Jack Nicklaus is the next best at 11 from 1970–80). Braid also had 17 consecutive top-10s, starting in 1896, matching Taylor for the all-time record.

Braid's Open victories came in 1901 at Muirfield, 1905 at St. Andrews, 1906 at Muirfield, 1908 at Prestwick, and 1910 at St. Andrews. The latter win made him the first to win five Opens, though Taylor later matched the total and Vardon reached six. Braid was the first player to shoot a round in the 60s in the Open, carding a 69 in the third round at Royal St. George's in 1904. His 72-hole record of 291 set in 1908 stood for 19 years.

For the last 45 years of his life, until he died in 1950, Braid was the head professional at Walton Heath, near London.

Opposite page and above: *A long hitter, Braid won five British Opens from 1901–10. "There is a special delight in seeing the kind of divine fury with which he laces into the ball," wrote golf historian Horace Hutchinson.*

In 1969, Carner became the last amateur (to date) to win an LPGA event, capturing the Burdine's Invitational in Miami. She turned pro the following season at age 30 and promptly won the Rookie of the Year Award.

JoAnne Gunderson Carner

Of the great players to come along in the post–World War II era, JoAnne Carner is the only one, male or female, who nearly remained a career amateur. Not turning pro until she turned 30, Carner won five U.S. Women's Amateur championships, a total second to only Glenna Collett Vare. She then went on to compile a pro record that placed her in the LPGA Hall of Fame. Carner, née Gunderson, is the only player to have claimed the U.S. Girls' Junior, Women's Amateur, and Women's Open titles. She won the junior championship in 1956, also reaching the final of the Women's Amateur that year at age 17. She went on to claim the amateur title in 1957, '60, '62, '66, and '68. In 1969, she won the Burdine's Invitational on the LPGA Tour; she's still the last amateur to win an LPGA event.

With prize money rising in the pro game and no worlds left to conquer in amateur golf, Carner decided to turn pro in 1970. The former "Great Gundy" earned a new nickname on Tour when her fellow pros tabbed her "Big Momma," mainly for her ability to launch the ball long distances. Carner's gregarious personality and go-for-broke style quickly made her a popular figure in the pro ranks.

Despite an aversion to practice, Carner compiled an impressive record on the Tour, winning the Vare Trophy for low scoring average five times, earning three Player of the Year Awards, and claiming three money titles. Her biggest victories came in the 1971 and '76 U.S. Women's Opens. From 1974–83, she ranked among the top five money winners in all but one year.

Despite her late start, Carner had a long stay near the top of the LPGA because she achieved more success after age 40 than any player of either sex ever has. Of her 42 LPGA Tour victories, 19 of them came in her 40s, and she led the money list when she was 43 and 44. She is the oldest player to win an LPGA event, having claimed the Safeco Classic at age 46.

"Big Momma" Carner wears her emotions on her sleeve, making her one of the most popular performers on the LPGA Tour.

Billy Casper

Below: *Casper (left) came from seven strokes back in the final round, and then defeated Arnold Palmer (center) in a playoff, for the 1966 U.S. Open title at the Olympic Club in San Francisco. Opposite page: Casper was renowned nearly as much for his girth as his golf game. "I have a furniture problem," he said late in his career. "My chest has fallen into my drawers."*

Billy Casper was never recognized for the golfer he was. It's difficult to say just why. It may have been the way he presented himself to the golfing public when he was in his prime. Perhaps, too, it was because he defeated one of the game's most beloved icons, Arnold Palmer, for a national championship.

In any case, from 1954, when he turned pro, through 1979, his last year on the regular PGA Tour, Casper won 51 tournaments to place sixth on the all-time winners list. His victories included two U.S. Opens (1959 and 1966) and a Masters (1970). He played on eight U.S. Ryder Cup teams, was a nonplaying captain for one other, and won the annual Vardon Trophy for low stroke average five times. He was twice the Tour's leading money winner, and in 1970 he became the second golfer in history to win more than $1 million in career prize money. He was twice the PGA Player of the Year and is a member of the PGA/World Golf Hall of Fame. By all accounts, he was one of the best players in American golf history.

William Earl Casper Jr. was born in San Diego in 1931. He was an early product of an outstanding junior golf program in his hometown, but he played his first golf, he once recalled, "over the rocky ground of my grandfather's ranch in New Mexico. It was very rudimentary, to say the least. In fact, it wasn't really a golf course at all." He entered his first tournament as a 13-year-old in San Diego. "It was during World War II," he

Casper and his caddie react to a miss of what would have been the winning putt at the 1970 Masters. In the subsequent playoff, Casper putted brilliantly en route to a five-stroke victory over Gene Littler.

said. "I entered as a 24 handicap and shot an 80. My entry fee was refunded. I just had a hot round, but the officials wouldn't buy that."

Casper attended the University of Notre Dame for a year, then opted to play professional tournament golf. He joined the PGA Tour in 1954, and two years later he won his first event, the Labatt Open. From 1957–71, he won at least once every year, and usually was a multiple winner. His best season in that regard was in 1968, when he won six times on the circuit. What's more, he would win 12 times on the Senior PGA Tour from 1982–89, including a U.S. Senior Open in 1983.

In assessing his career once, Casper said he would have been more popular had he not tried to emulate the unemotional, stoic demeanor of Ben Hogan. In private, Casper was a sharp-witted individual with the guile of a pool-hall sharpie. Indeed, he was an excellent pool player as a young man, a skill that transferred to his golf via an exceptional, even uncanny, ability to putt. In this he was unique. At address, his left hand rested against his left thigh and didn't go beyond it in the follow-through. The technique kept him from flipping his hands and resulted in a short, compact "pop" stroke that was highly effective for a long time. His putting skills helped him capture the 1970 Masters. Playing in an 18-hole Monday playoff with Gene Littler, Casper totaled six one-putt greens on the front nine to open up a five-stroke lead. He prevailed 69–74 for his first and only green jacket.

Casper's game from tee to green was distinguished by a slide into impact that seemed less than graceful, but perhaps only because he was always rather heavyset. Even as a young man, Casper was constantly fighting a weight problem, and at one point he became known more for an exotic diet of health foods than for his splendid game. Perhaps, too, his weight was off-putting to the galleries. Furthermore, upon examining his life outside of golf, he found it wanting in purpose and joined the Mormon church. Hence, a certain piety was added to his demeanor.

But his cardinal sin, as many seemed to consider it, was when in 1966 Casper came from seven strokes behind with nine holes to play to tie Palmer for the U.S. Open, played at the Olympic Club in San Francisco. Then, in the 18-hole playoff, Casper erased a two-stroke deficit with eight holes to play to win his second Open title. To be sure, Palmer played poorly on the back nine in both instances, but what people failed to note was that all the while Casper was shooting sensational scores—a 3-under-par 32 on the back nine of the championship proper and a 1-under-par 34 on that same nine in the playoff. Had he defeated anyone besides the immensely popular Palmer, Casper might have been extolled more for his achievement. In a sense, he was a victim of someone else's charisma.

Casper (right) and Gene Littler meet before the final round of the 1970 Masters. Casper's victory at Augusta was sweet redemption, coming a year after he blew the third-round lead and had to settle for second place behind George Archer.

Glenna Collett Vare

A contemporary of Bobby Jones, Glenna Collett Vare dominated women's amateur golf in the United States much the same way Jones did the men's game. Her enduring legacy is a record six U.S. Women's Amateur titles—this in a time when women's professional golf didn't exist. And, like Jones, she was an attractive champion who always conducted herself with class.

Collett was born in 1903 (one year after Jones) and played baseball in her youth before being introduced to golf at age 13 by her mother, who thought it a more appropriate game for a girl. She came under the wing of Scottish pro Alex Smith, a two-time U.S. Open champion who reputedly said, "If I can't make a champion out of her, I'll be a disgrace to the Smith family."

Vare was perhaps the longest hitter women's golf had ever seen. Asked later how she was able to outdrive her contemporaries, she said, "Very simple. I just hit the ball harder than they did." Collett won her first Women's Amateur in 1922. After a tough semifinal loss in 1924 (her semifinal opponent's winning putt on the first extra hole bounced off Collett's ball and into the hole), she claimed her second title in 1925.

In 1928, Collett began a streak that saw her win 19 consecutive matches in the U.S. Women's Amateur, carrying her to titles in 1928, '29, and '30; she lost in the final in '31. Collett also was runner-up in 1932. Oddly, she lost the '32 final to Virginia Van Wie, 10 & 8, even though she had defeated Van Wie by a then-record margin, 13 & 12, in 1928. Collett Vare, who married in 1931, won her sixth Women's Amateur in 1935, beating 17-year-old Patty Berg in the final.

Collett Vare won the Eastern Amateur and the North and South Amateur six times each, but the one big title she never claimed was the Ladies' British Open Amateur. She reached the final twice, losing in a memorable match to British great Joyce Wethered in 1929 and falling to relative unknown Diana Fishwick the next year.

Collett Vare thoroughly dominated women's golf in the 1920s, capturing four U.S. Women's Amateur championships. Inducted into the Women's Golf Hall of Fame in 1951, she is the namesake for the Vare Trophy, given each year to the player with the lowest scoring average on the LPGA Tour.

Harry Cooper

Below: *Cooper won two Canadian Opens and lost playoffs to Sam Snead in two others.* Opposite page: *In the 1936 U.S. Open at Baltusrol, Cooper shot 284, the lowest score in Open history at the time, only to be overtaken by late finisher Tony Manero, who shot 282.*

He finished with 31 official PGA Tour victories, but Harry Cooper might be most remembered for his near misses in the game's biggest events. Indeed, he has the most victories of any player who never won a major championship (and ranks 13th on the all-time win list). Twice he completed his final round as an apparent winner of the U.S. Open, but both times the tournament was snatched away by a later finisher.

Cooper was born in England in 1904, the son of a golf professional, but his family moved to Texas when he was a boy. He burst into the pro ranks quickly, winning the 1926 Los Angeles Open at the age of 21 and earning the nickname "Lighthorse Harry" because he played so quickly. Cooper's first U.S. Open chance came in 1927 at Oakmont. He three-putted the 71st hole from eight feet but still would have won outright if Tommy Armour, finishing an hour later, hadn't birdied the 18th hole to force a playoff. The 18-hole playoff was tied until Cooper took two strokes to escape a bunker and double-bogied the 16th hole.

In 1936, Cooper finished the U.S. Open at Baltusrol with what would have been a record total of 284, despite bogeys on two of the last five holes. He was congratulated on his victory, but unheralded Tony Manero was in the process of burning up the course on the way to a closing 67 for a winning total of 282.

Cooper led through each of the first three rounds in the 1936 Masters, but he closed with a 76 and finished second to Horton Smith. He was also the runner-up there in 1938 to Henry Picard. He never advanced past the semifinals of the PGA Championship and never returned to the isle of his birth to play in the British Open.

His second-place finishes notwithstanding, Cooper was one of the finest players of his generation. His best year was 1937 when he won eight tournaments, led the money list, and won the first Vardon Trophy. He captured the Canadian Open in 1932 and 1937.

Henry Cotton

The glory days of British golf seemed to have passed when Henry Cotton arrived on the scene in the 1930s. Once the sole province of Britain's Great Triumvirate (Vardon, Taylor, and Braid), the British Open had been claimed by players from the United States in every year from 1924–33. But Cotton became a British hero by claiming the title three times—in 1934, '37, and '48.

Cotton, born in 1907, was one of the game's first great practicers, along with his near contemporary in the United States, Ben Hogan. He came from a well-to-do family, but Cotton hit so many balls as a young man that his hands were often blistered, and he walked with a tilt due to spending so much time with his right shoulder lower than his left in the golf stance. He became a very straight driver of the ball, much like Hogan and Byron Nelson, and had a sound all-around game, though his putting was sometimes suspect.

Cotton broke through at the 1934 British Open at Royal St. George's. He opened with rounds of 67 and 65, phenomenal scoring for that era, and opened a nine-stroke lead (the "Dunlop 65" golf ball was named for his second round). A 72 in the third round stretched the lead to 10 strokes, and Cotton could afford to stumble in with a 79 and still win by five. His second Open title came at Carnoustie in 1937 when he shot a final-round 71 in a driving rainstorm to beat a field that included the entire U.S. Ryder Cup team.

A wonderful driver, Cotton struggled with his putter. "Golfers who have never known the agony and humiliation of the putting twitch," he said, "will, therefore, never quite know how to rank this disease in the list of golf's illnesses."

Cotton finished third in both 1936 and '38, then fourth in the first post–World War II Open in 1946. Turning 40 didn't slow him down. At Muirfield in 1948, he won his third Open, again on the strength of a great round, a second-round 66. He won by five strokes.

Though he played very little in the United States, Cotton was one of the first British pros to frequently compete on the European continent. Later, he became a noted teacher and writer on the game, eventually settling in Portugal.

Cotton holds the prized Claret Jug, symbolic of victory in the British Open, which he won three times. In 1933, the English star played a challenge match against American Walter Hagen. Hagen won 3 & 2 and collected a £100 side bet from Cotton.

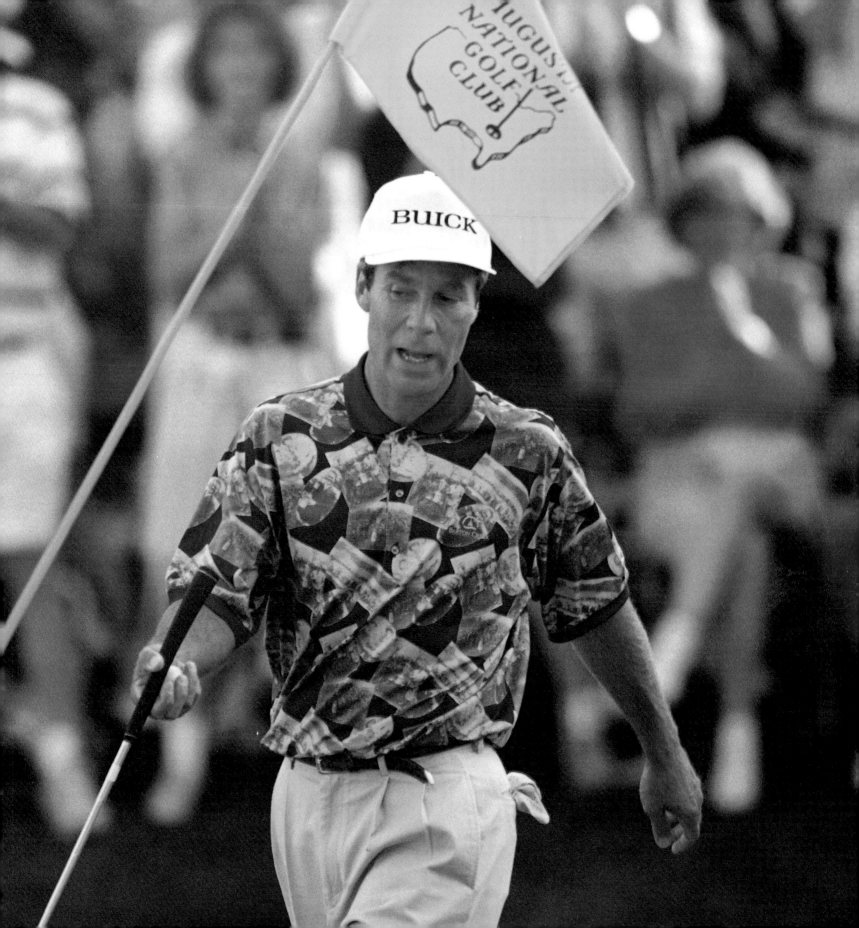

Ben Crenshaw

He came out of the University of Texas in 1973 with a long swing, a silky putting stroke, and an amateur portfolio that stamped him as the game's next great star. Today, Ben Crenshaw's swing is considerably shorter, and he has compiled an outstanding record as a professional while falling a bit short of the lofty peaks predicted of him. One thing remains the same: his sweet putting stroke.

Indeed, Crenshaw will go down in history as one of the greatest putters in the game. Thus, it is perhaps no surprise that his two major titles have come in the Masters at Augusta National, where putting is paramount. In fact, in addition to winning the Masters in 1984 and '95, he has two seconds, two thirds, and two fourths there.

Crenshaw grew up in Austin, Texas, and stayed in town to play for the Longhorns, winning an unprecedented three consecutive NCAA Championships in 1971, '72, and '73 (sharing the second with teammate Tom Kite). He seemed ready to take the world by storm when, in the fall of 1973, he won his first event as a member of the PGA Tour, the San Antonio-Texas Open.

Crenshaw was plagued by wildness off the tee, however, and didn't post his next win until 1976. He claimed three victories that year and finished second on the money list; both would remain career highs. Though he has been plagued by inconsistency throughout his career, Crenshaw had 19 victories through 1996 and had finished among the top 10 money winners seven times.

More than any other player, Crenshaw loves and respects the game's history, so the major championships are especially important to him. For his first decade as a pro, they brought nothing but frustration—two seconds at the Masters, two seconds at the British Open, a playoff loss at the PGA Championship, and a third-place finish at the U.S. Open. Finally, he broke through at the 1984 Masters. Crenshaw's win at the 1995 Masters was also an emotional one, coming a week after the death of his longtime teacher, Harvey Penick.

Opposite page: *Crenshaw dedicated an emotional Masters victory in 1995 to his late teacher, Harvey Penick.* Above: *Crenshaw frequently talks about the mental side of the game. "I'm about five inches from being an outstanding player," he once said. "That's the distance my left ear is from my right."*

Jimmy Demaret

The flamboyant Demaret, shown at Pinehurst in 1936, won three Masters and played for the United States on three Ryder Cup teams during his rollicking career.

Some years after he had quit the competitive golf scene, Jimmy Demaret was asked if he would have won more had he taken golf more seriously. His response was typically candid. "If I had," he said, "I wouldn't have won anything."

In point of fact, James Newton Demaret, born in Houston in 1910, took his golf quite seriously. After all, he won three Masters and 28 other tournaments on the PGA Tour, and by all accounts of his contemporaries was one of the best wind players the game has ever had. With his enormous hands, and from a stance in which his feet—even with a driver—were but a few inches apart, Demaret was a wizard at manipulating the golf ball. It's just that the times of golf gravity were interspersed, rather liberally, with times of frolic.

Indeed, it could be said that Demaret's vivacity and love of life gave as much to the game as did his wonderful playing talent. Perhaps more. Demaret, like most of his generation of golfers, got into the game as a caddie. When he joined the pro tour in 1927, all golfers wore the same style of clothing—brown or gray slacks, brown or black shoes, a white dress shirt, a tie, and sometimes a fedora hat. The clothing was not only conservative in color and cut, but the materials tended to be heavy and, in hot-weather locker rooms, "kind of stank," said Jimmy.

So one day in the late 1930s, while in New York City, Demaret visited a shop in the garment district where movie stars had their clothes made. There he saw bolts of lightweight materials in a kaleidoscope of bright colors that caught his eye. As Demaret remembered, he had acquired his taste for colors from his father, a house painter who, in the days before paints were mixed by machine, would mix by hand and test shades on the walls of his home. Jimmy asked if he could get some golf shirts and slacks made of such goods. Told the stuff was for ladies' garments, Jimmy

"Colorful" doesn't begin to describe Demaret. Chartreuse and ecru were among the hues he wore on Tour, leading one writer to label him "the affable eyesore of the professional golfing brigade." He became a more conservative dresser late in his career, after wild colors became standard attire.

said he didn't care, he wanted to play golf in them. His request was fulfilled, and a sartorial revolution in golf got under way. Not only did golfers begin to wear more lively looking clothing, but the clothes were lighter, and the shirts in particular made swinging a club easier.

It is difficult to measure precisely all other contributions to the game of golf Demaret made in his long career, because many evolved from his sunny disposition. He had an infectious smile, an even more jolly laugh, told jokes with a relish, and had the gift of a professional entertainer. As a young man, he sang at a Galveston, Texas, nightclub owned by a man who was his first sponsor on the pro tour. Demaret was never shy about adding his lilting tenor voice to a party. Golf quote books are peppered with Demaret witticisms. When Jimmy woke up one day and saw Pebble Beach covered with snow, he quipped, "I know I got drunk last night, but how did I wind up at Squaw Valley?" When one struggling golfer asked Demaret for advice, Jimmy shot back: "Take two weeks off—then quit the game."

Actually, in the days before golf was televised, Demaret was often asked to do radio play-by-play broadcasts of golf tournaments. He infused them with his elfin, improvisational spirit, the most memorable call coming upon the second shot Lew Worsham holed from 105 yards to win the Tam O'Shanter World Championship in 1953. "The damn thing went in the hole," Demaret reported. When television did come into golf, Demaret was on the ground floor. For five years, he was a witty and incisive commentator (with

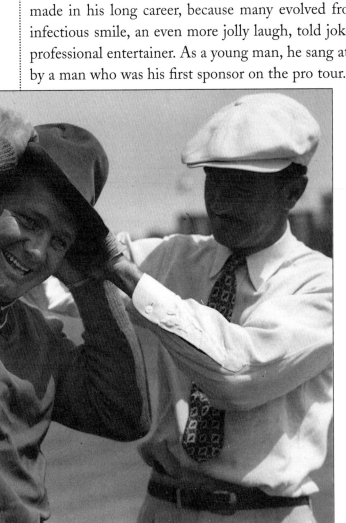

The 1940 Masters champion, Demaret hangs onto his "lucky hat" as runner-up Lloyd Mangrum tries to snatch it. Demaret also won the green jacket in 1947 and 1950.

Gene Sarazen) on the Emmy Award-winning television program *Shell's Wonderful World of Golf.* The show aired in the 1960s and had much to do with the growth of golf in the United States and around the rest of the world.

Demaret's association with the producer of the Shell show, Fred Raphael, led to the beginning of the Senior PGA Tour. Through Demaret's connections and influence, the made-for-television competition *Legends of Golf* hit the air in 1978 with the team of Sam Snead and Gardner Dickinson prevailing. Bringing back to legitimate competition famous Tour pros in their 50s and beyond, the tournament was the stimulus—the "father"—of the Senior PGA Tour. The first 12 tournaments were played at Onion Creek C.C. in Austin, Texas, on the course Demaret designed.

But perhaps Demaret's finest contribution to the golfing landscape is The Champions Golf Club in Houston, which he originated and owned along with his partner, Jack Burke Jr. The two courses—Jackrabbit and Cypress Creek—are both superb layouts. The latter held a Ryder Cup Match (1967), a U.S. Open (1969), and a U.S. Amateur (1995). Although he had input, Demaret didn't design the courses. However, he did leave his unique imprint on their environs. He made sure there were many colorful flowers trimming the grounds. Even more to the point, Demaret saw to the construction of a men's locker room that is the epitome of good fellowship—a warm and friendly place with a big and finely wooded bar, where golfers could spend many a sagacious hour talking the game and just having fun. A Demaret kind of place.

Above and below: *Demaret had many hard-fought battles with fellow Texan Ben Hogan. One of their best was at the 1949 Phoenix Open, when he defeated Hogan in a playoff. Three days later, Hogan suffered serious injuries when a bus slammed into his car near Van Horn, Texas. In 1950, Demaret appeared in the Ben Hogan movie* Follow the Sun.

Roberto De Vicenzo

Considering he is the greatest golfer ever from South America, it is unfortunate that Argentina's Roberto De Vicenzo is best remembered for his scorecard blunder that cost him a chance to win the 1968 Masters. The globetrotting De Vicenzo won somewhere in the neighborhood of 200 tournaments around the world, including eight in sporadic appearances in the U.S.

The one that got away came in Augusta in 1968 on De Vicenzo's 45th birthday, when he shot a magnificent 65 in the final round to apparently tie Bob Goalby for first place. But fellow competitor Tommy Aaron had marked a 4 instead of a 3 for De Vicenzo on the 17th hole, and the Argentinean signed the incorrect scorecard. Once De Vicenzo signed the card, he was stuck with the 4 on the 17th for a total of 66 and a second-place finish. Three weeks later, he won the Houston Champions International.

De Vicenzo's history at the British Open came to a better end, though for a long time it seemed he was destined to be a perennial also-ran there. In his first three attempts—in 1948, '49, and '50—he finished third, second, and third. He went on to also place third in 1956, '60, and '64. Finally, in 1967, De Vicenzo won the event at Hoylake, finishing two strokes ahead of Jack Nicklaus, to become the oldest British Open champion of this century (44). For good measure, he added yet another third in 1969.

De Vicenzo started humbly as a caddie's assistant at a course near his home in Buenos Aires. He quickly showed a talent for the game, and at 21 he won the Argentine Open and PGA. An international career soon followed. He was known

De Vicenzo's scorecard gaffe at the 1968 Masters has obscured his overall record. His greatest moment came in 1967 when he captured the British Open at Hoylake in England.

as one of the game's best ball-strikers, though sometimes a shaky putter. De Vicenzo collected national open titles like they were trinkets; so many, in fact, that no one is quite sure of the exact number (perhaps as many as 39, in 14 different countries). Though he never won the U.S. Open, De Vicenzo did capture the first U.S. Senior Open, in 1980.

A glum De Vicenzo (left) sits next to winner Bob Goalby during the trophy presentation at the 1968 Masters. Had he not signed an incorrect scorecard, De Vicenzo would have met Goalby in a playoff the following day. Instead, he settled for second place, one stroke behind.

GOLF LEGENDS OF ALL TIME

Chick Evans

*T*he legacy Charles "Chick" Evans left through his golf will continue to bear rich fruit for as long as the world remains civilized. It will far outdistance his achievements as a champion golfer, as superb as they were.

In addition to his talents on the golf course, Evans made a name for himself as the editor of Golfers Magazine, *which began publishing in 1902 and found a wide audience.*

Evans was born in 1890 in Indianapolis. When he was three, the family moved to Chicago, and this city would be identified with Evans for the rest of his long life. He began in golf as a caddie at the Edgewater G.C. on Chicago's north side, where in time he would become an honored member. Tall and slender, he soon developed a fine golf swing noted for its economy of movement, and by the age of 16 he was clearly marked for high achievement at the game.

In 1906, Evans qualified for the prestigious Western Amateur for the first time. He would take the title eight times, the first coming in 1909. In 1910, Evans reached another, higher level as a champion. He won the Western Open, in that era one of golf's major titles, defeating the best professionals in the game in doing so. No amateur would win this event again until 1985. In 1911, he won another highly regarded event, the North and South Amateur, and in that year added the French Amateur to his record.

In 1914, Evans came within inches of tying Walter Hagen at the U.S. Open when his pitch shot on the last hole just missed. In general, his annual quest for the national championships, the U.S. Open and Amateur, were invariably frustrating. A brilliant striker of the ball, especially with his irons, Evans was at best an erratic putter. In one event, before the club limitation rule was effected, he carried four putters in his bag. An extrovert with a bright smile, Evans liked being the center of attention. But for some reason he was hampered in his earlier days by a certain nervousness in the nationals. No less a figure than Harry Vardon once

An accomplished ball-striker, Evans struggled mightily with his putter—or putters. He became so discouraged at one point that he carried four of them in his bag. But his woes on the green rarely stopped him from contending in the prestigious amateur events of his era.

said Evans was the best amateur he had ever played with in the United States, yet the sandy-haired, freckle-faced Chicagoan could not get past the semifinals of the U.S. Amateur.

Finally, in 1916, the "uncrowned amateur champion" broke through. In June of that year, Evans won the U.S. Open at the Minikahda G.C. in Minneapolis with a record-setting score of 286, 2-under-par, that would hold up for the next 20 years. Then in September, at age 26, he defeated defending champion Bob Gardner in the final of the U.S. Amateur, at the Merion Cricket Club outside Philadelphia, to become the first player to win both national titles in one year. He would win the Amateur again in 1920, when he survived a 41-hole marathon in round three before trouncing the legendary Francis Ouimet in the finals.

Evans tees off in the 1936 U.S. Open at Baltusrol, 20 years after scoring a stunning victory in the Open at the Minikahda Club in Minneapolis. His winning score of 286 stood as the best in Open history for two decades.

With World War I underway in Europe, Evans used his celebrity in 1917 and 1918 to help raise funds for the Red Cross. To that end, he traveled some 26,000 miles to 41 cities playing exhibitions. But his social consciousness and sense of responsibility would reach their highest point beginning in 1930, when the Great Depression was beginning to take hold of the nation. Evans's fame had brought him many offers to endorse products and earn appearance money. Dedicated to amateurism (he quit caddying before his 16th birthday to preserve his amateur status, as the Amateur Code demanded in those days), he turned all money offers down. However, he was allowed to use monies received from the sale of his golf instructional phonograph records for the establishment of a caddie scholarship fund instituted in his name. It was meant for young male (and later female) caddies who could not afford a college education but qualified for one with good grades in high school.

Evans, 56 years old and long past his prime, adds to his trophy collection after winning a minor tournament in Chicago in 1946, seven years after he retired from national competition.

The first two Evans Scholarship recipients entered Northwestern University in 1930, and since that time the program has accounted for more than 5,000 college and university graduates from over 30 different schools around the country. The program has long been administered by the Western Golf Association, which raises the funds (over $5 million a year) through individual contributions and the Western Open. Many Evans Scholars have gone farther in life than they might have otherwise, because Evans never forgot his own rather humble beginnings and an appreciation of learning he inherited from his mother.

Evans formally retired from national competition in 1939. However, in 1962 he made an honorary 50th appearance in the U.S. Amateur, and he continued to compete in local Chicago tournaments. In the latter, he would appear with a thin golf bag over his shoulder containing 10 clubs (a number he advocated as enough, on the notion that more people could then afford to play golf), all of them extra long. In this, he was some 20 years ahead of the vogue for longer-than-standard clubs.

Nick Faldo

Above: *Faldo slips on the green jacket after defeating Scott Hoch in a playoff at the 1989 Masters.* Opposite page: *This fist-pumping episode at the 1992 U.S. Open belies Faldo's stoic approach to his craft.*

One day in 1990, Nick Faldo asked Ben Hogan how to win the U.S. Open. Hogan replied, "Shoot the lowest score." Faldo thought the great man was having a joke. He asked the question again. And got the same reply. End of conversation.

Faldo didn't really need to ask. His game was in the Hogan mold, a paragon of consistency derived from solid and well-understood swing fundamentals combined with unassailable concentration as well as an unquenchable thirst for practice. In fact, the very swing Faldo developed and which brought him to the pinnacle of the game has a certain Hoganesque quality: compact, controlled, and consistent.

If his parents had anything to do about it, Nicholas Alexander Faldo, born in 1957 in Hertfordshire, England, was going to be something special in something. His mother in particular had various visions of what her only child would become—an actor, a dancer, a clothing model, a concert pianist. She never had golf in mind, but that was the direction her strong-willed son chose. However, the training of the boy's mind to be very good at whatever he decided to do and be certainly took.

At age 14, after watching Jack Nicklaus play golf on television, Nick Faldo resolved he would give the game a go. A fine natural athlete—tall, well-built, and strong—he got the knack for the game quickly. He became a regular contender in British junior amateur golf, and in 1975 he won the British Youths and English Amateur championships. That led to a golf scholarship at the University of Houston, a perennial collegiate golf power. But after only 10 weeks on campus, Faldo decided that was not the way to advance his career, and he was in a hurry. He dropped out, returned home, and in late 1976 turned professional golfer. He was 19 years old.

In the mid-1980s, Faldo rebuilt his swing with the help of respected teacher David Leadbetter. The work paid off in 1987, when he won the British Open after parring each hole in the final round.

Faldo had some success early on playing the European PGA Tour, winning 11 tournaments from 1977–84, plus one on the U.S. PGA Tour. However, he discerned that if he was going to go to the very top, he would have to make some major changes in his swing. Working closely with South African teaching professional David Leadbetter, Faldo completely revamped his technique. It took a full two years to bring the changes up to speed. In 1985 and '86, he won nothing in either Europe or the U.S., where he played periodically. Then, everything he had been working on fell into place. In 1987, Faldo won the British Open, making 18 pars in the final round to catch and pass a faltering Paul Azinger. Mr. Consistency.

Faldo's star had now completely cleared the horizon, and his accomplishments began to multiply. In 1988, he won twice in Europe and lost in a playoff with Curtis Strange for the U.S. Open. Then in 1989, he captured his second major title, the Masters, after a playoff with Scott Hoch. He won four other events that year on the European Tour. In 1990, Faldo again won the Masters, and again in a playoff (with Raymond Floyd), to become only the second successful defender of that much-prized title. That same year, he tied for third in the U.S. Open and then won his second British Open crown. He won his national championship a third time in 1992.

For all his great success over a 10-year stretch, Faldo became dissatisfied with his game. There were uncharacteristic lapses in his concentration and his shot-making. They may well have been related to the breakup of his marriage, from which three children were born and which was treated by the scandal-mongering element of the British press with particularly disgusting venom.

In any case, Faldo went back to his drawing board for swing and playing adjustments and decided to play full-time on the U.S. PGA Tour, which he felt was the most competitive in the world. The decision paid dividends almost immediately. In 1995, he won the Doral-Ryder Open, a mini-major in that it is played on a difficult course and always has one of the strongest competitive fields. Then in 1996, he won his third Masters.

A self-possessed man with an acerbic wit

Above: *Faldo kisses the Claret Jug after winning the 1990 British Open, the same year he became the first foreigner to win the PGA Player of the Year Award.* Below: *In 1995, Faldo moved his base of operations to the United States, and in 1996 he won his third Masters.*

that put off the golf press, yellow and otherwise, Faldo's success has often been questioned. In making 18 pars to win his first British Open, some speculated he didn't *want* to win so much as to simply let others falter and hand him the prize. He won his first Masters when

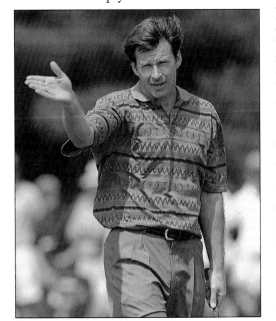

Hoch missed very short putts, his second when Floyd unaccountably pulled a 7-iron approach shot into the water beside the 11th green. In his third Masters victory, Greg Norman handed it over by shooting a final-round 78.

In making 18 straight pars, it wasn't as if he didn't try to make a birdie or two. No putts dropped. Against Hoch, he fired a final-round 65 at Augusta National and won in sudden-death with a birdie. Against Floyd, Faldo had a last-round 67 to Floyd's 72. Against Norman, Faldo had a brilliant final-round 69 on a course playing as difficult as it ever has. How then might Faldo answer his detractors? He won because he shot the lowest scores.

Raymond Floyd

Raymond Floyd's father was a career Army man, and his son's march on the golf course mirrors his being raised on military bases—back absolutely straight and head high at attention, like a good soldier.

Raymond's carriage may have had something to do with the golf swing he developed. Tall but with rather short arms and a heavily muscled upper body, Floyd created what even he would acknowledge was a peculiar looking swing. It has been likened to the construct of a football linebacker, or perhaps a windmill with a screw or two loose. The club goes back rather sharply to the inside with a dip of his left shoulder, then is raised seemingly straight up to the completion of the backswing. The zigzag route is pretty much repeated going back to impact.

Had he not stood so tall at address, the swing might have been more fluid and formful. Floyd's response to comments about his swing has always been, with a sly smile, "It ain't how; it's how many." Exactly. And if he'd tried to shape a golf swing in the "classic" mode, he might well have taken too many. In a game where less is more, Raymond Floyd got well onto the lesser side of the ledger, and he has stayed there far longer than the pattern of his golf swing would suggest possible.

Clearly, Floyd simply has a gift for the essence of the game, keeping the ball in play and finding a way to make a score. Floyd was an excellent baseball pitcher, his performance in his high school days so impressive that he was offered a $30,000 bonus to sign with a major-league club. He opted for golf, a game he was inspired to play

Opposite page: Floyd has been a Tour fixture since the early 1960s. His first professional victory came at the 1963 St. Petersburg Open, and he and Sam Snead are the only golfers to win Tour events in four decades. Below: Floyd receives the green jacket from Jack Nicklaus after winning the 1976 Masters.

by his father and for which he also had obvious potential. And yet, early on, he almost threw his gift to the winds.

One golf observer once said it was a wonder Floyd made it in golf when his first "heroes" were Doug Sanders and Al Besselink, two older fellows and outstanding golfers who had a penchant for wine, women, and song. Floyd would later recount that his first 12 years as a touring pro (he began on the circuit in 1963) were "just a means to an end," a way to

Right and below: Floyd has always had the ability to hit the ball a long way, especially in his early days on Tour. His problem was lack of accuracy. "It got so I hit so many balls out of bounds," he once said, "that they had to put the (golf ball) factory on the night shift to keep me supplied."

make enough money to have fun elsewhere. He was also a notorious high-stakes gambler on his golf game. The consensus of the golf community in the early 1970s was that Floyd's talent was going to waste, even though he had won a PGA Championship (1969) and four other Tour events, and would never bear full fruit.

Then he met his wife, Maria, a strong personality in her own right who had a more conventional set of values. Everything was turned around. Raymond Floyd would become such an esteemed figure in golf that he would become known simply as Raymond. Everyone knew who was meant. In 1975, having gone four years without a victory and with the first of his three children just born, Floyd won the Kemper Open. He followed that up in 1976 with an astounding eight-shot victory in the Masters as well as a win in the World Open. From 1977–92, he won 15 times, including another Masters, another PGA Championship, and the U.S.

Open in 1986, which gave him the distinction of being, at 44, the oldest-ever winner of the national championship.

Floyd had a knack for winning the big ones, the tournaments with the best fields playing on the toughest courses. Along with his major victories, Floyd won the 1981 Tournament Players Championship, the 1982 Memorial, and the Doral-Ryder Open three times. The last Doral victory, in 1992, came just eight months before his 50th birthday, and it prepared him well for his entry to the Senior PGA Tour.

Floyd was expected to be a terror on the Senior circuit, and he definitely made that calculation a sound one. Right out of the box, late in 1992, he won three times, including the Senior Tour Championship, a senior major. He won twice in 1993 and four times in '94, including another Senior Tour Championship. In all, through 1995, Floyd had won

34 times on both the PGA and Senior PGA Tours. And just to show the young bucks of the next generation that he still could keep up, he entered 14 events on the PGA Tour from 1993–95 and finished in the top 10 three times—and nine times in the top 25.

Floyd, who won the 1983 Vardon Trophy for low stroke average (70.61), played on eight Ryder Cup teams and was non-playing captain of another. Floyd is also one of just two golfers to win tournaments on the PGA Tour in four different decades. The other one? Sam Snead.

Floyd gets some advice from fellow Tour superstar Greg Norman. Renowned for his ability to sink high-stakes putts, Floyd often ranked among the scoring leaders on Tour. He won the Vardon Trophy in 1983 with an average of 70.61 shots per round.

Ralph Guldahl

$H$is up-and-down career is one of the great mysteries of golf, but for a few years in the late 1930s Ralph Guldahl was the best player in the game. The 6'3" Texan is one of only six players to win back-to-back U.S. Opens, claiming the title in 1937 and '38. He was second in the Masters both of those years, winning it in 1939. And he won the Western Open, then one of the game's big events, in 1936, '37, and '38. Then his game suddenly vanished—for the second time.

Guldahl first emerged in 1932 when he won the Arizona Open at age 20. He nearly won the 1933 U.S. Open, missing a four-foot putt on the 72nd hole to finish one stroke behind Johnny Goodman. Then he went into a slump and quit the Tour in frustration in 1935. After changing his grip and spending long hours practicing, Guldahl returned in 1936 and led the Tour in scoring average.

Guldahl beat Sam Snead by two strokes at Oakland Hills in 1937 to take his first U.S. Open title. He eagled the 8th hole and birdied the 9th, then learned he could beat Snead with a 37 on the back. "If I can't play this last nine in 37 strokes," he said, "I'm a bum and don't deserve to win the Open." Guldahl shot a 36 on the back to finish with a 69 and set a new U.S. Open 72-hole record of 281. The next year, at Cherry Hills, Guldahl also closed with a 69 to win by six strokes. At the Masters in 1939, Guldahl beat out Snead by one stroke with another final-round 69.

Guldahl won a couple tournaments in 1940, but the next year he struggled greatly. He took motion pictures of his swing and compared them with his swing when he won the Masters, but he couldn't find the fatal flaw. All he knew was that the winning touch had vanished. His enthusiasm for the game gone, Guldahl left the Tour in 1942 and, except for brief periods, never returned.

Opposite page: *The mercurial Guldahl is pictured in a happy mood in 1939 as he prepares to defend the U.S. Open titles he won in 1937 and '38.* Left: *Though long past his prime, Guldahl kept in the spirit of things at the 1950 Western Open.*

Walter Hagen

Walter Hagen was effectively the first American professional golfer—not golf professional, professional golfer. He made his living only by playing the game. When Hagen did take his one and only head-pro job at a club, at the Oakland Hills C.C. outside Detroit, it was while the course was under construction. When it opened for play, he quit the post. It was not for Walter Hagen to stand for hours in the sun giving golf lessons; to spend his time in a small, cluttered shop selling clubs, balls, and tees; to be an underling in the employ of anyone. That was a brave way to go in the first decades of the 20th century, when golf was still new to the United States and there was only the merest beginnings of a tournament circuit.

Did Hagen foresee a time when many men might follow his lead? Probably not. Hagen was simply dancing to his own inner music. Still, in his daring Hagen had set a precedent. It was not to be followed by too many in his time, but he initiated the notion that an outstanding golfer could make his way in the world by showing off his talent to the public eye. As Herb Graffis, a pioneer golf periodical publisher, put it in 1980: "Today's [Tour] pros should light a candle every day of their lives in the memory of Walter Hagen." And because Hagen was such a colorful personality, he also got the game of golf on its way as a significant sporting pastime among the populace at large.

Above: *A friend of many in the golfing community, Hagen poses alongside three-time Western Open winner Macdonald Smith (left) and singer Bing Crosby (center). Opposite page: Hagen's trophy collection included two U.S. Opens, four British Opens, and five PGA Championships.*

How did Hagen do it? It wasn't with his long game. With his long, loose swing, he was often wild off the tee and inconsistently accurate even from the fairways. Nevertheless, Walter played at the highest level from 1914–36. During that 22-year period, Hagen won

Had the athletic Hagen picked baseball instead of golf, he might have been teammates with legendary pitcher Grover Cleveland Alexander.

a total of 44 events, including two U.S. Opens, four British Opens, and a record-setting five PGA Championships, four of them in a row (1924–27). He did it with a vivid imagination when in trouble—an eye for finding a gap in the trees and a gift for fitting a ball through it—plus a magnificently deft touch as a chipper and putter. Just as important, he had not a doubt at all of his ability. Playing one of the most frustrating of games, he never let golf get him down. His "philosophy" of golf was expressed in a couple of simple homilies: If you find yourself hooking the ball on a given day, just aim to the right a little more; also, he expected to miss seven shots per round and didn't fret when they occurred.

While the majority of Hagen's victories were at stroke play, his forte was as a match-play competitor. In this *mano-a-mano* format, he was a master psychologist who, for one thing, knew full well that his disorderly tee-to-green game made him seem like easy pickings for the purer ball-strikers, but who would be rendered limp, if not angry, by Hagen's amazing recoveries from trouble. Adding to that was the brio with which he pulled off his miracles. He also understood the effect of pressure on athletes. In this regard, Hagen's most memorable remark came when he was told, while preparing to spend a night on the town on the eve of the final match for the 1926 PGA Championship, that his opponent, the nervous Leo Diegel, was already in bed: "Yes," said Hagen, "but he isn't sleeping."

Walter Hagen reflected a classic American success story, the athlete playing his way out of humble circumstances. He was born in 1892 in Rochester, New York, the son of working-class German immigrants. His father, a blacksmith, advised his son to learn a trade and thought his boy a "bullhead" for passing up car-

pentry. As a youth, Hagen was an excellent ice skater and baseball player. His first athletic sights were set on playing major-league baseball, and in a tryout with the Philadelphia Phillies in the winter of 1912, he received a very favorable review. But he also had been playing golf, beginning as a pre-teen caddie. During the summer after his baseball tryout, he tied for fourth in the second golf tournament he had ever entered, the U.S. Open. When he won that championship the next year, his future was settled.

What set Hagen apart, aside from his athletic gifts, was his instinct and flair for showmanship. "Barnum and Bailey rolled into one," said Graffis. But Hagen somehow gave his "circus act" a kind of salon quality. He had a way of walking with his head tilted up, like royalty, that—along with the lifestyle he developed—would earn him the lifelong sobriquet "Sir Walter."

His son, Walter Jr., once suggested that his dad's love of the high life came from the days when his father caddied at the Country Club of Rochester for such people as George Eastman (founder of Eastman Kodak) and other wealthy, sophisticated people. Hagen was beguiled by the talk he heard of travel and the high life. Watching from a respectable distance as the club members danced away summer evenings, the young Hagen was entranced. He did not resent the

Left: Hagen compensated for erratic drives with an impeccable short game. Here he finds himself in a familiar spot: chipping from the rough. Below: Hagen enjoyed the fruits of his labors. "I don't want to be a millionaire," he once said. "I just want to live like one."

rich; he simply wanted a piece of their action. In Walter Jr.'s words: "It set Dad's standards. He always wanted a look of success." Walter Sr. put it another way, memorably: "I don't want to be a millionaire; I just want to live like one." He did just that.

And yet, for the silk shirts, tailored knickers, jeweled cuff links, and other accoutrements associated with the high life that Hagen fancied, he also projected the down-to-earthiness of the common man. Certainly the ordinary citizen golfer could identify with Hagen's unkempt, razzmatazz golf. He stood at the ball with the wide stance of a home run hitter, made a rainbow-arc swing that ended with an unfettered lunge, sprayed shots all over the lot, and was consistently flirting with danger—from which he recovered with insouciant aplomb. Furthermore, with Hagen there was none of the dour gravity brought to the game by the Scottish pros who emigrated to the United States and were golf's first showcase players in the country. Hagen was a joy to watch because he obviously enjoyed

Whether battling in a professional tournament or playing in a casual foursome, Hagen enjoyed himself. "You're only here for a short visit," he once said. "Don't hurry. Don't worry. And be sure to smell the flowers along the way."

what he was doing. He never complained about a golf course—he called them all "sporty little layouts"—and as a friend once remarked, he "never had a temper."

It was an intriguing combination Hagen put together, and through it he was a major factor in the growth of American golf. In the period when he was most active as a golfer, the pro tour was in its embryonic state and paid little in purse money. Hagen earned most of his money playing exhibitions, some 4,000 18-hole outings from 1914–41 that brought in an estimated $1 million. This was an impressive sum for the

Near the end of his career in 1940, Hagen tees off during a practice round for the PGA Championship at Hershey (Pennsylvania) Country Club. He died of throat cancer in 1969.

time, but what made it all the more so was that Hagen did not perform for preset fees and expenses. He barnstormed, playing to whatever size audience he could draw, usually at a dollar a ticket. And Sir Walter did not restrict himself to playing in established golf country. He also traveled to the hinterlands—the Dakotas, Wyoming—where the courses were usually quite primitive and where he had to pull in every golf fan and curiosity seeker within a 500-mile radius.

Hagen satisfied one and all, and he never slowed down the proceedings with dry dissertations on the mysteries of the game. He was the Johnny Appleseed of American golf. No one can say for certain how many persons Sir Walter inspired to take up golf, but a fair guess is that he corralled one for every dollar he made on the exhibition circuit alone, not counting their sons and daughters.

Sandra Haynie

Though overshadowed by the great Kathy Whitworth, Sandra Haynie was one of the best and most consistent players in the women's game from 1961–75. Haynie enjoyed her biggest moments in the sun in 1974, when she won the U.S. Women's Open and LPGA Championship. She is one of only three players to sweep those events in a single year (along with Mickey Wright, 1961, and Meg Mallon, 1991).

Haynie beams after capturing her first victory on the LPGA Tour, a one-stroke win over Mickey Wright in Austin, Texas, in 1960. She won her second Tour event the following week.

Haynie was born in Fort Worth, Texas, and made a fast start in the game by winning the Texas Amateur in 1958 (at age 15) and '59. She turned pro in 1961 and claimed her first victory in 1962 at age 18. Haynie won at least one tournament every year for 14 years starting in 1962, claiming 39 titles in that span. She finished in the top five on the money list 11 times and was second five times. Though Haynie never earned the money title, she took Player of the Year honors in 1970.

Her best year, however, was 1974, when she captured a career-high six victories, including the only two major championships then contested. First, she beat JoAnne Carner by two strokes to win her second LPGA Championship (the first came in 1965). Then, at La Grange Country Club outside Chicago, Haynie pulled off one of the most dramatic finishes in U.S. Women's Open history. She birdied the last two holes to win by one stroke, sinking a 75-foot putt on the 17th and a 15-footer on the 18th.

Hampered by arthritis and knee surgery, Haynie retired twice and successfully came back each time. After sitting out most of 1977–80, she won three events in 1981 and 1982, finishing second on the money list the latter year. Sidelined again from 1985–87, Haynie returned for 1988 and '89 to surpass $1 million in career earnings before calling it quits for good. Haynie finished with a total of 42 victories, tied with Carner for seventh best all time. The Texan was known primarily as a very straight driver and steady player, hitting fairways and greens with regularity.

Haynie won at least one Tour event for 14 consecutive seasons (1962–75), after which she began to suffer from chronic arthritis. Injuries to her back and knee also slowed her late in her career, but they didn't diminish her place in history. She became the eighth member of the LPGA Hall of Fame when she was inducted in 1977.

Harold Hilton

Below and opposite page: Hilton broke John Ball's stranglehold on the British Amateur with consecutive victories at the turn of the century. Later he wrote several widely read books, including the instructional manual Modern Golf. *He was enshrined in the PGA/World Golf Hall of Fame in 1976.*

*E*nglish amateur Harold Hilton, whose career of winning major championships spanned the years 1892–1913, holds several significant distinctions. He is the only British player to ever win the U.S. Amateur, one of three amateurs to win the British Open (along with John Ball and Bobby Jones), and one of four to take the U.S. and British Amateurs in the same year (along with Jones, Lawson Little, and Bob Dickson).

Hilton's earliest triumphs came in the British Open. At age 23, he won the 1892 Open at Muirfield, the first time the tournament was played at 72 holes. Five years later, Hilton captured the Open at his home course, Royal Liverpool. Trailing James Braid by three strokes after 54 holes, Hilton posted a closing 75 for a total of 314 and retreated to the clubhouse to play billiards while Braid tried to beat his score. Hilton emerged to watch Braid make a 4 at the last hole when he needed a 3 to tie. Late in his career, Hilton nearly added a third Open title. Also, he was one stroke out of a playoff in 1911, a year in which he would meet success elsewhere.

Hilton was developing a reputation as better at stroke play than match play, having lost in the final of the British Amateur in 1891, '92, and '96. But he went on to win by an 8 & 7 margin in the 1900 final over James Robb and reclaimed the title in 1901. After a dry spell, he took his third and fourth British Amateurs in 1911 and 1913.

In 1911, at age 42, Hilton decided to make the overseas trip to America to try to win the U.S. Amateur. His appearance attracted much attention in the American press, and Hilton rolled to the final against Fred Herreshoff. The Englishman lost a 6-up lead before winning with a par on the 37th hole.

Hilton stood just 5′6″. He took such a fast and furious swing that he often came up on his toes at impact and lost his hat at the finish. Nevertheless, he was a very accurate player.

Ben Hogan

*B*en Hogan's career in golf was a saga of overcoming, one that is legendary in its proportions. He grew up in difficult financial circumstances, and more significantly had to live with the calamity of his father's suicide. A basic swing flaw took him years to overcome. When he found the solution, he lost more time serving in the armed forces. Then, Hogan barely survived a devastating highway accident from which he suffered physical pain the rest of his life. But Hogan persevered to become one of golf's all-time great champions, not to mention one of the game's most intriguing personalities.

Opposite and below: *After nearly losing his life in a car crash, Hogan returned to the pinnacle of golf, winning the 1951 U.S. Open at Oakland Hills. His playoff-round 67 ranked with the greatest rounds of his career.*

William Ben Hogan was born in 1912 in Stephenville, Texas, and was raised in nearby Dublin until the age of 10, when his father Chester took his own life. Following that tragic event, Ben's mother moved the family (Ben and his older sister and brother) to Fort Worth, where Ben, at age 12, learned of golf as a caddie and found his lifework.

As a teenager, Hogan clearly had enough innate ability to consider a future as a golfer, but it did not come easily. Extremely private, he did not socialize well, which kept him from the networking that helps start careers and move them forward. And, being small of stature, Hogan developed an extended golf swing in order to create power. He achieved the power but at the expense of accuracy. Hogan's driving, in particular, featured a wild hook that for the first eight years of his professional career (he turned pro at age 18) kept him on the periphery of the tournament circuit. Hogan concluded in subsequent years that the most important shot on any golf hole is the first one, the drive, and he eventually became exceptionally accurate off the tee while retaining sufficient power. What's more, he added

GOLF LEGENDS OF ALL TIME

Hogan lost to Sam Snead (left) in an 18-hole playoff at the 1950 Los Angeles Open. "I'm only scared of three things," Snead once said. "Lightning, a sidehill putt, and Ben Hogan."

to that a stunningly precise approach-shot game that made up for a lifetime of relatively ordinary putting skills.

Hogan often said he figured the golf swing by himself—"dug it out of the dirt," as he liked to put it. He took the idea of practice to an extraordinary level for golfers of his era, and while this surely was an important element in his success, he was also an inquisitive student of the golf swing who picked up ideas on technique from many sources, one of which was Henry Picard, a Masters and PGA champion in the 1930s who would become one of golf's best teachers. Picard convinced Hogan that to beat his hook, he had to "weaken" his left-hand grip by turning the hand more to the left. Seemingly overnight, Hogan's basic shot became a left-to-right power fade, a trajectory that came to be known as the "Hogan Fade." The flight pattern would influence how the game would be played from then on.

In early 1940, Picard's lesson hit home. Hogan won his first professional tournament individually, the much prized North and South Open. (In 1938, he had shared victory with partner Vic Ghezzi in the Hershey Four-Ball.) The next week, Hogan won the Greater Greensboro Open, and later in this "coming out" season he won twice more. After nine years of struggle, during which he more than once had to leave the tournament circuit for lack of funds, Hogan was at last fulfilling his promise. From 1940–42, he won 15 tournaments, and in each year he was the Tour's leading money winner. All that was missing on his increasingly impressive résumé was a major title.

Hogan was primed for this breakthrough, but it was put on hold with the advent of World War II. The Tour was discontinued in 1943, and that year Hogan was inducted into the U.S. Army and then assigned to the Air Corps. Like most celebrated athletes serving military duty, Hogan did not see combat. He trained pilots for a time but, for most of his hitch, played exhibitions to raise money for the war effort, played casual golf with high-ranking officers, practiced on his own, and entered the occasional Tour event when the circuit began again in 1944. Still, he was away from steady, high-level competitive golf for 3½ years.

When Hogan returned full-time to the tournament circuit, he made up for lost time with characteristic tenacity. In his first outing after his discharge, in the fall of 1945, Hogan won the Portland Invitational with a record-setting 72-hole score of 261—27-under-par. Then from 1946 through early 1949, playing what he would later describe as the best golf of his life, he won 32 tournaments, including his first and second majors—the 1946 PGA Championship and 1948 U.S. Open.

Then, after playing four events on the 1949 winter circuit and winning twice, Hogan along with his wife, Valerie, nearly lost their lives. On a foggy two-lane highway outside Van Horn, Texas, a Greyhound bus traveling in the opposite direction moved out to pass a slow-moving truck and collided head-on with Hogan's car. When Hogan saw the accident coming, he instinctively stretched across the front seat to protect his wife. He saved her from serious injury, and saved his life, for at impact the steering column of his car was rammed into the driver's seat. Nevertheless, Hogan's left collarbone was fractured, his left ankle was snapped, and many of his internal organs were severely damaged. His face

New York honors Hogan with a ticker-tape parade after he won the 1953 British Open, his third major championship of the year.

Conserving energy became a priority for the intense Hogan, who entered just a handful of tournaments each year from 1951–53. Yet he continued to practice with fierce determination, and to overwhelm the competition.

was smashed into the dashboard, which led to a gradual diminishment of the vision in his left eye. He would intimate, after he retired, that he had essentially played the last three or four years of his competitive golf career with sight in only one eye.

Furthermore, during his recuperation time, Hogan's life was again seriously threatened by a blood clot. A deft operation saved him, but his legs were left in a permanent state of weakness and disrepair. That he survived at all was a wonder. That he would, within a year, return to competitive golf was beyond anyone's farthest consideration. But it happened, and in a most dramatic fashion.

In January 1950, Hogan entered his first competition following the accident, the Los Angeles Open, and nearly won it; he lost to Sam Snead in a playoff. But the most astounding moment came in June 1950. In the U.S. Open, which at the time concluded with a 36-hole final day, Hogan barely held on to tie George Fazio and Lloyd Mangrum with a par on the last hole. In the 18-hole playoff the next day, Hogan won the title.

Had he never played competitive golf again, Hogan's extraordinary comeback in 1950 would have been enough to secure his place forever in golf annals. But he would expand on it, and mightily. Cutting back his playing schedule to preserve his strength,

Hogan entered an average of only six tournaments a year from 1951–53, most of them the majors except for the PGA, which was then a physically grueling match-play event requiring as much as two full rounds a day. Nonetheless, during that period Hogan won eight times, five of them majors—two more U.S. Opens, two Masters, and one British Open in his only attempt for that crown. In 1953 alone, he won what might be called golf's Triple Crown—the U.S. and British Opens and the Masters. He would also play on the U.S. Ryder Cup team, captain the team for a third time, produce an especially influential instructional book—*The Modern Fundamentals of Golf*—and found a golf equipment manufacturing company in his own name.

Hogan won his last tournament in 1959, the Colonial Invitational. In 1960, at age 48 and essentially retired from competitive golf, he had enough left to be in a position through 71 holes to win his fifth U.S. Open. That he lost did nothing to tarnish a reputation for golf skill and a will to excel that will live through the ages.

Said Hogan: "One of the greatest pleasures in golf—I can think of nothing that truly compares with it unless it is watching a well-played shot streak for the flag—is the sensation a golfer experiences at the instant he contacts the ball flush and correctly."

Hale Irwin

*O*nly four players—Willie Anderson, Bobby Jones, Ben Hogan, and Jack Nicklaus—have won more U.S. Opens than the three claimed by Hale Irwin. In fact, along with those four (who won four Open titles apiece), Irwin is the only other man with more than two. He took the national championship in 1974, '79, and '90, in the latter year becoming the oldest man, 45, to take the title.

It is fitting that the U.S. Open, where conditions are most difficult, should represent Irwin's crowning achievement; he has always been at his best on tough courses. Among his 20 PGA Tour victories, he has won on such renowned courses as Harbour Town, Butler National, Riviera, Pinehurst No. 2, Muirfield Village, and Pebble Beach. He is a relatively short hitter, a fine long-iron player, and a tough competitor; he is at his best when par is a good score.

Irwin, a native of Missouri, fueled his competitive drive as a football player at the University of Colorado, where he was an all-conference defensive back. He also won the 1967 NCAA golf championship. Irwin joined the Tour in 1968 and had two career wins before the 1974 U.S. Open. Irwin emerged there, surviving the "Massacre at Winged Foot," to win with a 7-over-par total. He won his second Open, at Inverness, at even par.

Irwin's third Open win came in very different fashion. He was tied for 20th place, four strokes behind, entering the final round, but closed with a 67 that included a sizzling 31 on the back nine at Medinah. A 45-foot birdie putt on the 18th hole ultimately put him in a playoff with Mike Donald, which Irwin won with a sudden-death birdie on the 19th hole.

Though he didn't win any other majors, Irwin was one of the top players in the game for a long period. He won at least once in all but two years from 1973–85 and finished among the top 10 money winners eight times in his career. He made 86 consecutive cuts from 1975–78, the third-best streak in history.

Opposite page: *A competitive PGA Tour player in his 40s, Irwin dominated the seniors when he turned 50, winning more than $1.5 million in 1996.* Above: *Irwin agonizes over a missed putt at the 1990 U.S. Open. He went on to defeat Larry Donald in a tense 19-hole playoff.*

GOLF LEGENDS OF ALL TIME

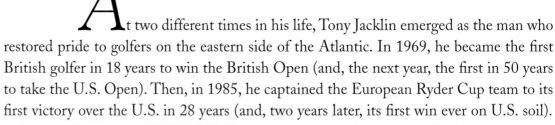

Tony Jacklin

Below and opposite page: Jacklin was only 25 years old when he romped to victory in the 1970 U.S. Open at Hazeltine National. He overcame 40-mph winds in the first round to shoot 71, then followed with three consecutive 70s to defeat Dave Hill by seven strokes.

At two different times in his life, Tony Jacklin emerged as the man who restored pride to golfers on the eastern side of the Atlantic. In 1969, he became the first British golfer in 18 years to win the British Open (and, the next year, the first in 50 years to take the U.S. Open). Then, in 1985, he captained the European Ryder Cup team to its first victory over the U.S. in 28 years (and, two years later, its first win ever on U.S. soil).

Born in Scunthorpe, England, Jacklin turned pro in 1961 at age 17. He became a strong force in 1967, winning two events in Britain and finishing fifth in the British Open. The next year, he came to America to play the PGA Tour and won the Greater Jacksonville Open, the first U.S. Tour victory by a British-based player since Ted Ray won the 1920 U.S. Open.

In 1969, Jacklin became a British hero by winning the British Open at Royal Lytham and St. Annes, beating Bob Charles by two strokes. Jacklin's performance in the 1970 U.S. Open was even more impressive; his seven-stroke victory margin at Hazeltine National was the largest since 1921.

Jacklin finished fifth, third, and third in the next three British Opens, but, thereafter, was never a factor in the major championships. Some think the 1972 British Open was a fatal blow. He seemed primed to win there before a reversal of fortune at the 71st hole. Tied for the lead with Lee Trevino, Jacklin watched Trevino chip in for a par and then three-putted from 15 feet for a bogey. Jacklin won once more in the U.S., in 1974, and became less of a factor on the European Tour as the decade wore on.

Jacklin, an outspoken and confident sort, found a new role in the 1980s as captain of the European Ryder Cup team. Working with a strong nucleus of players, he instilled a belief that the Europeans could beat the mighty U.S., and, after coming close in 1983, they accomplished the trick in 1985 and 1987.

GOLF LEGENDS OF ALL TIME

Bobby Jones

The sum total of Bobby Jones's contributions to golf is virtually all-encompassing. As a championship golfer, he set standards that still hold, even if the scores he shot have become irrelevant. He was an excellent and prolific writer on golf—particularly his golf instruction, which has a clarity, intelligence, and warmth of insights that to this day makes good reading. He was the quintessential amateur during his competitive career—an impeccable gentleman (once he "grew up") and true to the code of amateurism. Finally, he gave his game a golf course and a tournament that have become institutions reflecting what has come to be considered the ultimate expression of golf aesthetics and competitive rigor and drama.

Robert Tyre Jones Jr. was born in Atlanta in 1902, the only child of a lawyer who as a young man was an excellent baseball player, and became an inveterate golf buff. Bobby began playing golf at age five, and he was soon deemed a prodigy. For good reason. At nine, Jones won the junior championship of the Atlanta Athletic Club, soundly defeating a lad seven years older than himself in the final match. At 12, Jones won three different club championships, in one shooting a final-round 73. He won the Georgia State Amateur the next year, then played in his first U.S. Amateur, where he took the defending champion, Bob Gardner, on the 31st hole before losing.

With his Amateur showing, Jones impressed one and all with his golf, but not with his temper. He was a club and tantrum thrower, the misbehavior accompanied often by highly "colorful" language. He would ever pleasure in such language when in private and among men friends, but he did lose the tantrum part, which got in the way of his progress as a golfer. In the third round of his first British Open, in 1921, Jones was playing poorly and picked up at the 11th hole without finishing it. It was a breach of good conduct he never forgot, and it had much to do with the princely deportment for which he became renowned.

Above: *Jones became the quintessential sportsman. "You might as well praise a man for not robbing a bank," he said, "as to praise him for playing by the rules." Opposite page: "The real way to enjoy playing golf," Jones said, "is to take pleasure not in the score, but in the execution of strokes."*

Jones and his wife, Mary, arrive in New York after Bobby won the 1926 British Open at Royal Lytham. Later in his glorious career, the denizens of New York honored him with a ticker-tape parade through Manhattan.

In view of the tournament schedule of many amateur golfers today, which includes heavy summer schedules and extensive and highly competitive collegiate play, one of the most remarkable aspects of Jones's career was that he played so little competitive golf. He studied mechanical engineering at Georgia Tech, earned a degree in English literature at Harvard, and —after 18 months at the Emory University Law School—took the Georgia state bar examination. He passed it and left school to practice law. He never did play college golf.

Preferring to play himself into condition for each golf season, Jones did not practice much on the range. He only rarely entered amateur events, other than the nationals. He won the Southern Amateur three times, but he has no record in such long-time prestigious amateur tournaments as the North and South or Western. He did play in two pro tour events in preparing for his monumental 1930 season: the Savannah Open, which he lost by a shot to Horton Smith, and the Southeastern Open, which he won by 13 strokes after finishing double bogey, par, double bogey. Other than those few instances, the national championships were his only interest, and his metier.

During what has been described as his eight "fat years," 1923–30, Jones won the U.S. Amateur five times (and lost once in the final), the U.S. Open four times (lost twice in a playoff), the British Open three times (in four tries), and the British Amateur once (in three tries). He became known as Emperor Jones, and even hard-nosed professionals who managed to beat him in an Open counted it a high achievement, if not an honor.

Jones definitely had a sense for historic accomplishment, for prior to the 1930 season he resolved to win all four of the then-major golf titles in that one year—the U.S. and British Open and Amateur championships. It had never been done before, and this would be his last chance for he had also decided that 1930 would be his last year of competitive golf. He had a family to raise, and he never did get over the edgy nervousness that his youthful temper displayed. The physical and emotional stress of his great play over the previous 15 years was taking its toll. Furthermore, the Walker Cup was being played in Great Britain in 1930, which allowed him the opportunity for his goal. Except in one instance, he had only played in Great Britain when representing the U.S. as a Walker Cup player, and the bulk of his travel expenses were covered by the USGA.

And so it came to pass that one of the finest feats of sustained golfing excellence in the history of the game took place: the Grand Slam. Or as one wordsmith of the day phrased it: the "Impregnable Quadrilateral."

Said Jones: "Getting in a water hazard is like being in a plane crash—the result is final. Landing in a bunker is similar to an automobile accident—there is a chance of recovery."

It is certain Jones was after the British Amateur crown, for it was the only one of the four majors he had never won. Jones's most anxious moment in the British Amateur, at St. Andrews, was in the fourth round, when Cyril Tolley had a 12-foot birdie putt on the last hole to win 1 up. He missed, and Jones won on the first extra hole after laying a stymie on his foe. Jones breezed in the final, however, clubbing Britain's Roger Wethered, 7 & 6. At Hoylake two weeks later, all ears were tuned to Jones as the British Open was broadcast over American radio for the first time. Jones led the Open through the first three rounds and broke the 72-hole course record by

10 strokes. When he arrived back in the States, New Yorkers honored him with a ticker-tape parade.

On to Minnesota and the U.S. Open, the third leg. At the Interlachen Country Club, Jones took a five-shot lead with a third-round 68—the lowest he had ever shot in the U.S. Open. Nevertheless, he had to birdie three of the last six holes in the final round to win by two over Macdonald Smith. A 40-foot birdie putt on the last green was the clincher.

Given his own momentum, and the undoubted awe everyone had for Jones by the time the U.S. Amateur came around, his victory in that championship was practically assured. Jones won

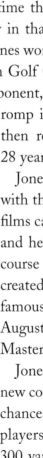

Right: *Jones is pictured at the 1930 British Open at Hoylake, the second leg of what one writer dubbed his "Impregnable Quadrilateral." Below: Jones accepts the 1930 British Open trophy after shooting 291 and breaking the 72-hole course record by 10 strokes.*

the 36-hole qualifying medal at Merion Golf Club in Pennsylvania with 69–73. In the matches, he was never down to any opponent, and he clinched the title with an 8 & 7

romp in the finals over Eugene Homans. Jones then retired from championship golf. He was 28 years old.

Jones, though, would long remain associated with the game. He made a series of instructional films called *How I Play Golf,* wrote several books, and helped design a set of clubs. Working with course designer Alister Mackenzie, Jones also created what would become one of the most famous layouts in the world—the course at Augusta National Golf Club, future home of the Masters.

Jones clearly articulated his criteria for the new course. It would give the average golfer a fair chance, while requiring the utmost from top players. To that end, there would be over 300 yards difference between the championship and members tees. But most significantly, the fairways would be wide, there would be no rough, and the course would include only 29 bunkers. The correct placement of shots would be paramount to negotiating the undulating ground. For Jones, golf was mainly a game of control.

Construction began in early 1932, with Jones hitting many shots from the projected tees and fairways to ascertain the proper angles, sight lines, distances, and playability of each hole. Many features of the Old Course at St. Andrews, Jones's favorite, were incorporated into the design. The grand opening was on January 13, 1933. People came from around the world for the unveiling. The weather didn't cooperate but golf was played, and Jones, on January 14, shot a round of 69. Augusta National had been properly christened.

With his place in history firmly established, Jones retired from championship golf at age 28. No one before or since has won four major championships in one year.

Robert Trent Jones

The most prolific and influential golf course architect of the second half of the 20th century, Robert Trent Jones is credited with designing more than 450 courses in 42 states and 23 countries in a career that has stretched over 60 years.

Jones was born in England in 1906 and moved to the United States with his parents in 1911. Jones knew early in life what he wanted to do. As a student at Cornell University, he designed his own curriculum of courses that would prepare him for a career in golf architecture. Jones then became a partner of Canadian architect Stanley Thompson.

Jones's career took off after World War II, when golf began to boom in America. He became known for his redesigns of U.S. Open courses, which he modernized to keep up with advances in golf equipment. The first and most famous of these redesigns came at Oakland Hills in preparation for the 1951 U.S. Open. The course was dubbed "The Monster," and Jones's reputation was established. He remodeled several other Open sites in the 1950s and '60s, and he eventually had three Opens played on courses of his own design: Bellerive, Hazeltine National, and Atlanta Athletic Club.

Jones advocated the philosophy of strategic design, blending the heroic and penal principles of golf architecture. He became known for designing courses with long teeing grounds and large, undulating greens, and he brought water into play more than the architects of past eras. His more famous courses include Spyglass Hill in California, Firestone in Ohio, the Dunes in South Carolina, Peachtree in Georgia, and Mauna Kea in Hawaii. He has worked extensively in Europe, where his most acclaimed course is Valderrama in Spain.

Jones, working with chief assistant Roger Rulewich, continued turning out courses as he approached his 90th birthday. The Robert Trent Jones Golf Trail in Alabama, opened in the early '90s, is one of the most ambitious and successful public-course projects in the country. Jones's sons, Robert Jr. and Rees, are respected architects in their own right.

Above and opposite page: Designer of more than a dozen Top 100 American courses, Jones culminated his career with the Robert Trent Jones Golf Trail in Alabama, a network of public courses that included Oxmoor Valley in Birmingham (pictured).

A winner of five majors in her career, King played a tournament for the ages at the 1992 LPGA Championship, where her 17-under-par 267 marked the lowest winning score in the history of major-championship golf, male or female.

Betsy King

*I*t took Betsy King a while to hit her stride on the LPGA Tour, going her first seven years without a victory. Once she came into her own, however, King needed only 12 productive years to put together Hall of Fame numbers.

King's lack of early success on Tour was a bit surprising in light of her amateur record. She finished eighth in the 1976 U.S. Women's Open as an amateur and led her Furman team to the national collegiate championship that year. King ranked among the top 30 money winners five times in her first seven years on Tour, yet she couldn't find the winner's circle.

Finally, three years of work with instructor Ed Oldfield began to pay off. King not only scored her first victory in 1984, but she added two more that year and won the money title and Player of the Year honors. King would again sweep those honors in 1989 and '93, also claiming the Vare Trophy for low scoring average in 1987 and '93. King won at least two tournaments every year from 1984–92, and she ranked among the top 10 money winners each year from 1984–95.

King won her first major title in the 1987 Nabisco Dinah Shore. She had her best year in 1989, winning six tournaments. The biggest was the U.S. Women's Open at Indianwood in Michigan, where King held or shared the lead after every round. King won the Nabisco Dinah Shore and U.S. Women's Open a second time each in 1990. King's best performance came in the 1992 LPGA Championship, where she shot rounds of 68–66–67–66 for an LPGA Tour-record 267 total and an 11-stroke victory.

As King approached the 30-victory mark required for induction into the LPGA Hall of Fame, the wins became harder to achieve. She finished second five times in 1993 before scoring her only victory, the 29th of her career, in the season's final event. After a winless 1994, King finally scored her 30th win in June 1995 at the ShopRite Classic. That year, she became the first LPGA player to pass the $5 million mark in career earnings.

Putting has not been King's strong suit. In 1995, for example, she led the LPGA Tour in birdies and top-10 finishes but failed to crack the top 40 in putting average.

Tom Kite

While he has earned nearly $10 million in a quarter-century on Tour, Kite views golf more as a recreation than an occupation. "Golf has never been work for me," he said. "You don't work golf. You play it."

*C*onsistency has always been the hallmark of Tom Kite's game. From week to week and year to year, his performance has seldom wavered. His reward is more than $9 million in PGA Tour earnings, second to Greg Norman on the career list.

Kite came out of Austin, Texas, a year ahead of Ben Crenshaw (they shared the same teacher, Harvey Penick, and also shared the 1972 NCAA Championship). Kite joined the PGA Tour in 1973 and established a pattern by making 31 of 34 cuts. While a steady money earner, it took Kite a while to become a winner, with just two victories through 1980.

Kite's breakthrough year came in 1981, even though he won only one tournament. He had a phenomenal 21 top-10 finishes in 26 starts, led the money list, and won the first of two consecutive Vardon Trophies. With the exception of 1988, Kite would win at least one tournament in every year from 1981–93, including three in 1989 (when he won his second money title) and two in 1984, '92, and '93, running his career total to 19 victories. He slipped out of the top 10 money winners only three times in that 14-year stretch.

For much of his career, Kite's only shortcoming was his inability to win a major championship. He finally earned his first in the 1992 U.S. Open, where he shot an even-par 72 on Sunday at Pebble Beach when most contenders were being blown away by severe winds. His best chance before that came in the 1989 U.S. Open at Oak Hill, where he led through three rounds before finishing with a 78. He was a perennial contender at the Masters for a long stretch, with 10 top-10 finishes from 1975–86 and finishing second in 1983 and '86.

At a slender 5'8", Kite isn't able to overpower courses, though he gets more distance off the tee than his frame might suggest. He has an excellent short game and for much of his career was one of the top putters, but he has struggled on the greens in recent years.

GOLF LEGENDS OF ALL TIME

Lawson Little

Although his professional career was considered a disappointment, Lawson Little dominated amateur golf for a two-year stretch more than any player in history except for Bobby Jones. In fact, in winning both the U.S. and British Amateurs in 1934 and '35, Little accomplished a feat unmatched by even Jones.

Little, born in 1910 in Newport, Rhode Island, first attracted attention in the 1929 U.S. Amateur. After Johnny Goodman scored a shocking upset of Jones in the first round, Little beat Goodman in the next round. Little reached the semifinals of the 1933 U.S. Amateur, earning a spot on the U.S. team for the 1934 Walker Cup at St. Andrews. He won both of his matches there, then stayed in Scotland for the British Amateur at Prestwick.

Little's performance in the 1934 British Amateur final is one of the finest days of golf ever played. He won the scheduled 36-hole match by a record margin of 14 & 13 over Jack Wallace, playing 23 holes in 10-under 4s. Returning to America, Little rolled to the U.S. Amateur title in another lopsided final, beating David Goldman, 8 & 7. The margins were closer in the following year's final matches—1 up over William Tweddell in the British Amateur, and 4 & 2 over Walter Emery in the U.S. Amateur. But when the championships were done, Little had won 31 consecutive matches to sweep the world's major amateur titles two years running.

Little turned pro in 1936 instead of trying for what would today be called a "three-peat." He won the Canadian Open that year, but his shining moment as a professional came when he defeated Gene Sarazen in a playoff to win the 1940 U.S. Open. However, that was the only major he won as a pro, and he collected only eight pro victories in all.

The stocky Little was one of the longer hitters of his day. He was also known for a fine short game, which was helped for a time by carrying as many as 26 clubs before the USGA imposed a 14-club limit.

GOLF LEGENDS OF ALL TIME

A long hitter and deft iron player, Little considered the mental aspects of golf to be as important as his physical skills. "It is impossible to outplay an opponent you cannot out-think," he said.

Gene Littler

His rhythmic swing and unerring accuracy earned Gene Littler the nickname "Gene the Machine." Hailed as one of the game's coming superstars in the mid-1950s, Littler went on to a long and successful career that included 29 PGA Tour victories over a span of 23 years. His only disappointment was that he won only one major championship, the 1961 U.S. Open.

Littler was born in San Diego in 1930 and first made an impact in the game when he won the 1953 U.S. Amateur. Still an amateur in 1954, he won his hometown event on the PGA Tour, the San Diego Open. Shortly thereafter, he turned pro. Littler's "golden boy" reputation was furthered when he finished second in the 1954 U.S. Open, missing an eight-foot putt on the 72nd green that would have gotten him into a playoff, and won four times in 1955. Littler slumped for a couple years, but he had his best year in 1959 with five victories.

The biggest win of his career came two years later when he took the U.S. Open at Oakland Hills. He came from three strokes behind by shooting a final-round 68. Littler came close in two other majors, losing in playoffs at the 1970 Masters to boyhood friend Billy Casper and the 1977 PGA Championship to Lanny Wadkins. At the latter event, the 47-year-old Littler was trying to become the second-oldest major-championship winner ever (Julius Boros won the PGA Championship at 48), but he lost a five-stroke lead on the back nine.

Littler finished among the top 32 money winners every year but one from 1954–75 (ranking second in 1959 and '62). The lone exception was in 1972 when he underwent surgery in the spring for cancer of the lymph glands. He was back in action six months later and won a tournament the next year. In 1975, at age 45, he won three times and finished fifth on the money list. His final PGA Tour victory came at age 47. He has gone on to add eight official and eight unofficial Senior PGA Tour wins.

Opposite page: "Gene the Machine" tees off at his first professional tournament in 1954. Above: Littler's career was interrupted in 1972 when he underwent surgery for cancer of the lymph system. He returned to win five more events before joining the Senior Tour in 1981.

Locke follows the flight of his ball, which invariably was right of center. The South African was never a popular player in the United States. American pros gave him the uncomplimentary nickname "Muffin Face" and criticized him for his slow play and unorthodox style.

Bobby Locke

Few foreign golfers have had as much impact on American golf as South Africa's Arthur D'Arcy "Bobby" Locke. In fact, no other international player has had such immediate success in the U.S. as Locke enjoyed after arriving in 1947.

Two developments in 1946 encouraged Locke, then age 29, to give the American Tour a try. He finished second to Sam Snead in the British Open, then beat Snead in 12 of 16 matches when the American star went to South Africa for an exhibition tour. Locke racked up six victories in 13 U.S. events in 1947, finishing second on the money list despite not playing the whole season. In 1948, he won twice, one of them by a Tour-record 16 strokes at the Chicago Victory Championship.

The run of victories was startling considering Locke's unorthodox methods. Early in his career, Locke had been a very short hitter; his solution for gaining distance was to hit a pronounced hook off every tee. He practiced very little and believed that American pros were too mechanical with their swings; Locke played by feel. Locke was a brilliant putter, but even on the greens he incorporated a sort of hook stroke.

The American pros resented both his success and the appearance fee he commanded to skip the British Open to play in George S. May's All-American Open in 1947, which he won. Locke also alienated the press by asking for $100 if they asked questions of an instructional nature. Ultimately, the PGA banned him in 1949, saying he had failed to honor commitments. They reinstated him in 1951, when Locke scored the last of his 10 American victories, but he played very little in the U.S. after that except for the U.S. Open.

Locke spent the latter part of his career playing mostly in Great Britain, and he won the British Open in 1949, '50, '52, and '57. Though he never won the U.S. Open, Locke finished third there in 1947 and '51, fourth in '48 and '49, and fifth in '54. He won the South African Open nine times.

"My approach to golf," Locke said, "is that I always play to beat the course. Even in match play, I do not concentrate primarily on beating my opponent."

Nancy Lopez

Golf is not a game conducive to streaks. Just making two or three consecutive birdies is something special, and it is rare for a golfer to win just two tournaments in a row. So when someone does streak, it gets a lot of attention. That's what happened to Nancy Lopez in 1978, when she won five events in succession on the LPGA Tour—and nine tournaments in all that year.

The streak hoisted Lopez immediately into the spotlight of big-time golf, and it also was a much needed fillip for the women's tournament circuit, which was having trouble at the time getting attention in an increasingly diverse sports world. Nancy's streak put her, and her organization, indelibly on the sports map. It didn't hurt that she also had one of the most beautiful smiles seen in a public figure, a smile that reflected the natural warmth of her character.

Nancy Lopez was born in 1957 in Torrance, California, but was raised in Roswell, New Mexico. Her father, Domingo, was the driving force behind Nancy's career. He was himself a golfer, and when he recognized Nancy was also

Above: *Lopez, pictured early in her career, joined the LPGA Tour in 1977 and won 17 of the first 50 tournaments she played in. Opposite page: Lopez celebrates sinking a $50,000 birdie putt in the inaugural LPGA Skins Game in 1990.*

interested and had talent, he did all he could to help her go forward in the game. Mr. Lopez made a modest living running an auto repair shop, but he always found the dollars it took to get his only child the golf equipment she needed—as well as to pay the greens fees at the local municipal course and military base course on which she learned to play.

There was no money for lessons, so Nancy was largely self-taught. The result of this was an unusual, idiosyncratic swing in which she arched her wrists to an almost vertical

Above and right: *Lopez honed a smooth swing, a steady putter, and a fierce competitive streak. "Competitors take bad breaks and use them to drive themselves that much harder,"* she said. *"Quitters take bad breaks and use them as reasons to give up."*

position to begin her backswing, which was very upright. From there on, however, she had a fine tempo and—with superb control of the club—had a "traditional" downswing and follow-through. Her distance was never outstanding, but she knew how to handle problem shots. Her father didn't give her much swing instruction, but when Nancy was eight he gave her a 4-wood as her first club and encouraged her to not tee the ball up but rather play the ball as it lay, as she found it. Lopez's soft putting touch, one of the best the game has ever seen, was probably innate.

It came together quickly. When Nancy was 12, she won the New Mexico Women's Amateur championship. That she defeated much older and more experienced golfers goes without saying. She was quickly deemed a golfing prodigy and was invited to play and practice as often as she liked at country clubs in Roswell. She took up the offers graciously. With that marvelous smile. Lopez won the U.S. Girls' Junior championship in 1972 and '74 and the Mexican Women's Amateur in '75. That same year, she entered her first U.S. Women's Open and tied for second. Within the above time frame, she also fit in three victories in the prestigious Western Girls' Junior championship. In 1976, she played for the U.S. Curtis Cup team and was also on the U.S. World Amateur team. Lopez received a golf scholarship to Tulsa University, but after her sophomore year she turned professional, in 1977.

All the more remarkable for an athlete of her accomplishments, Lopez—the wife of baseball star Ray Knight—found the time and energy to become a mother of three children, and to raise

them conscientiously. Her first daughter was born in 1983, her second daughter in 1986. Within those years and up to 1991, when she gave birth to her third daughter (and won a tournament while carrying her), Lopez won 19 tournaments, earned over $2 million in prize money, and had a stroke average of just over 71.

Lopez continued to play a full schedule of tournaments from 1992–95, teeing it up in 77 LPGA events, winning three of them, and collecting over $1 million in prize money. In the 1992 Rail Charity Classic, she tied her career-low score, a 64, in the final round to take the title. Through 1996, Lopez had won 47 official LPGA tournaments (plus three unofficial ones), which ranked her sixth all-time. The only LPGA players to win more often played in the formative years of the Tour, when there were fewer competitors.

In 1987, Lopez was inducted as the 11th member of the LPGA Hall of Fame. But in a curious parallel with Sam Snead, an unquestionably great player who never won the U.S. Open, Lopez has never been able to capture the women's national championship, although she has been runner-up on three occasions. She can't explain that one smudge on her otherwise splendid record, just as Snead couldn't. Nor has Lopez tried very hard to fathom the reason. "Maybe some day," she has said with that incandescent smile, which has defused all further questions on the matter. Some day she may win the Open, but if not she will not be any less a champion.

Lopez had 17 Tour wins by age 22 and was the second player in LPGA history to surpass $3 million in earnings.

Lloyd Mangrum

With his riverboat-gambler looks and stylish game, Lloyd Mangrum was a popular and successful player in the decade after World War II, although he was overshadowed by contemporaries Ben Hogan and Sam Snead. Mangrum ranks 10th all time in PGA Tour victories with 36, collecting 30 of those from 1946–54.

Mangrum grew up in Texas and turned pro at age 15 in 1929, but he didn't hit the Tour until the late 1930s. He first made news in 1940 when he scored his first victory at the Thomasville Open and shot a first-round 64 in the Masters (an 18-hole record that wasn't matched for 25 years or broken for 46) before finishing second.

Mangrum joined the Army in World War II and earned two Purple Hearts for being wounded during the Battle of the Bulge. He won the first postwar U.S. Open in a tense playoff over Byron Nelson and Vic Ghezzi. All three players shot 72s in the 18-hole playoff, necessitating another 18 holes. Mangrum shot another 72, while the other two had 73s.

In 1948, Mangrum began winning in bunches. He had seven wins that year, then added four in 1949, five in '50, four in '51, two in '52, and four in '53. He led the money list in 1951 and won the Vardon Trophy in 1951 and '53. In 1949, he was part of the longest playoff in PGA Tour history, going 11 holes with Cary Middlecoff at the Motor City Open before darkness arrived and the two were declared co-winners.

The 1946 U.S. Open remained Mangrum's only major victory. His next best chance came in the 1950 U.S. Open, where he and George Fazio lost a playoff to Ben Hogan. Mangrum trailed by one stroke on the 16th green when he lifted his ball to blow a bug off of it. Cleaning your ball on the green was then not allowed, so he drew a two-stroke penalty and ended up losing by four. Mangrum was a perennial contender in the Masters, finishing in the top eight every year from 1947–56, including a second in 1949.

Cary Middlecoff

Walter Hagen once called Cary Middlecoff one of the best ball-strikers to ever come out of American golf. Middlecoff won two U.S. Opens (1949 and 1956) and lost another (1957) in a playoff against Dick Mayer. He won one Masters title (1955) and had two seconds at Augusta National. He reached the finals of the 1955 PGA Championship and in all had 40 wins from 1945–61, which puts him in a seventh-place tie for all-time Tour wins with none other than Hagen. Middlecoff also had 30 second-place finishes, 23 thirds, and 181 top-10s. His first important victory came in the 1945 North and South Open, an auspicious accomplishment in that he was an amateur at the time and still a lieutenant in the U.S. Army.

Emmett Cary Middlecoff was born in 1921 in Halls, Tennessee, the son of a dentist. He attended the University of Mississippi and played on the school's golf team, then went into the military during World War II, serving as a dentist. Middlecoff would share his father's practice on and off for a time after his discharge from the Army, but he was encouraged by his father to give professional tournament golf a try. "Doc" Middlecoff joined the pro Tour full-time in 1947, but he would occasionally work at dentistry to keep up his skill should the golf not work out. As it happened, after 1948, he never filled another cavity other than those on golf courses.

Middlecoff (left) succeeded Sam Snead (right) as Masters champion in 1955. Middlecoff holed an 82-foot putt for an eagle-3 on the par-5 13th hole in the second round.

A tall, slender man, Middlecoff had an intense, nervous manner that seemed unsuited for a game that prizes calm and patience. But he found a way to counter his nature, purposely developing a swing technique that distinguished him from the great majority of golfers—a distinct pause at the top of his backswing. Middlecoff was also one of the more deliberate players in the game, fidgeting over the ball at address for some time before

Bob Jones described Dr. Emmett Cary Middlecoff (he disliked the name Emmett so he went by his middle name) as a "voluntarily unemployed dentist." Middlecoff spent two years as an Army dentist before being discharged as a captain.

beginning his swing. Joked writer Dan Jenkins: "A joke on the Tour used to be that Cary gave up dentistry because no patient could keep his mouth open that long." Actually, Middlecoff's slow play was mainly because of physical problems that plagued him for most of his career.

Though standing 6'2", the lanky Middlecoff had a compact swing from the tee. He was known for his approach shots, his ability to make crucial putts, and his slow play.

Middlecoff was born with an extra lumbar vertebrae. And while in dental school, standing for long periods in a dentist's position, he developed back problems. Golf exacerbated the condition. He also had trouble with his left eye, the result of a piece of Carborundum coming off a disc while treating a patient in the Army. It hit him in his left eye, which became ulcerated and was never the same again. He always wore a green visor on the golf course to kill the glare of the sun. On top of the physical problems, Middlecoff suffered from hay fever, beginning in 1955. "One of the main reasons I took a lot of time over the ball was that I couldn't see very well," Middlecoff recalled. "The hay fever was part of it, and the problem with the left eye was also a factor." Finally, he had to give up the game in the 1960s when he couldn't control the yips.

Middlecoff was always described as a "streaky" player, punctuating stretches of relatively ordinary golf with rounds—if not weeks and years—when he was at the pinnacle of his profession. For example, in winning his one Masters title, he outdistanced the second-place finisher, Ben Hogan, by seven shots. In winning his first U.S. Open, he bunched his best play—a second-round 67, a third-round 69—to take a three-shot lead into the last 18 holes. In defending his U.S. Open crown in 1957, Middlecoff got hot with two 68s in the last two rounds to force a playoff with Mayer. The 136 total tied a record for the final 36 holes of the championship.

On a bigger scale, Middlecoff in 1951 became a member of an elite group of golfers—including Hogan, Byron Nelson, Sam Snead, and Arnold Palmer—when he won three consecutive events. He

Middlecoff gave up his dental practice and, a year and a half later, won the 1949 U.S. Open at Medinah. "I was enough of a neophyte not to know what I was doing," he said. "I found out it was harder after that."

also had a knack for sustaining excellent, winning golf over a full year. In 1949, he won seven times on the circuit, including a dramatic U.S. Open in which he fended off Snead and Clayton Heafner by one stroke. He won six times in 1951 and matched that record again in 1955. Middlecoff played on three U.S. Ryder Cup teams (1953, '55, and '59) and in 1956 won the Vardon Trophy with a stroke average of 70.35. Middlecoff's last victory, at the Memphis Open, came in 1961 in his hometown. As an author, he wrote the insightful books *Advanced Golf* and *The Golf Swing*.

For all his obvious high achievements, Middlecoff was not sufficiently recognized as the golfer he was. To date, he has not been inducted into any of golf's Halls of Fame. This may be due in part to the fact that he was in his prime when Hogan and Snead were dominating figures, and personalities, in American golf. Be that as it may, Middlecoff's record speaks for itself. He was listed as the ninth best American golfer of all time, according to the 1989 PGA Tour rankings.

Johnny Miller

Johnny Miller first came to national attention as a golfer in the 1966 U.S. Open, at the Olympic Club in San Francisco. A tall, slender, blond 19-year-old with an exciting style, he put on a fine show of golf on national television as he finished as low amateur and in a four-way tie for eighth place. That he had the advantage of being a member of the Olympic Club was only coincidental. Miller looked the part of a "comer" on golf's biggest stage, and indeed he would become one of the game's lead players.

Born in 1947 in San Francisco, John Laurence Miller was directed into golf by his father at an early age. Under the tutelage of teaching professional John Geertsen, Miller developed a swing technique that would be adopted by a number of star players who came

Right: Because he was so accurate with his irons, Miller was capable of tremendous hot streaks. His closing 63 at the 1973 U.S. Open—the lowest round in Open history—featured nine birdies and one bogey. Opposite page: Miller shares a moment with his amateur playing partner, former President Gerald Ford.

after him—an "early set," in which he cocked his wrists very early in the takeaway and then completed his backswing. It made him one of the most accurate iron players the game has ever had. In 1964, Miller won the U.S. Junior Amateur championship, then went on to play college golf at Brigham Young University. In 1968, he won the highly competitive California Amateur title, then the following year turned professional and joined the PGA Tour.

Miller's third victory as a pro was the 1973 U.S. Open. An outstanding accomplishment in itself, especially at so early a stage in his career, Miller did it in stunning fashion, shooting a phenomenal and historic final round of 8-under-par 63 on the very difficult Oakmont C.C. course. Rains had softened the layout, mak-

ing the greens more receptive than usual, but a 63 in a U.S. Open had never before been achieved. It brought Miller from six shots off the 54-hole pace to win by a single shot, and it made him an instant star.

The following year, Miller solidified his status by winning eight events on the PGA Tour. Of his total of 24 career PGA Tour victories, eight would be in Arizona and Palm Springs, California (Phoenix Open twice, Tucson Open four times, Bob Hope Classic twice), in some cases with exceptionally low scores. Two of his Tucson victories came with 72-hole totals of 263 and 265. As a result, he was categorized as someone who played his best only in the "desert." In fact, the so-called

Right: Miller enjoyed playing at Pebble Beach, where he won three times. Here he exults after sinking a putt during the AT&T Pebble Beach National Pro-Am in 1987. Below: Miller won the AT&T in 1994, seven years after his previous Tour victory.

"Desert Fox" won nationwide and worldwide and on a geographically wide spectrum—Florida, the Carolinas, northern California, New York, Pennsylvania, and Europe.

Miller's second major title was the 1976 British Open, at Royal Birkdale in England. His best showings in other majors were two near-misses in the Masters. In 1971 at Augusta, Miller had a two-stroke lead after 68 holes but went 4-over the rest of the way to finish in a tie for second with Jack Nicklaus. Charles Coody won. Then in 1975, Miller fired a brilliant final-round 66 and needed a birdie on the last hole to tie Nicklaus. It was one of the more thrilling of Masters, but it was not to be for Miller. He tied for second with Tom Weiskopf.

There was a notable gap in Miller's victory production from 1977–79, when he won nothing on the PGA Tour and only once abroad. Many felt his attention had been distracted by the many endorsement and exhibition opportunities that came his way after making his mark. Indeed, he was one of the first modern-day professional golfers to become an agent-directed off-course commodity.

But Miller also involved himself deeply in raising a large family (six children, all two years apart), and he was beginning to suffer from a neurological problem with his knees that would gradually deteriorate to where he could play only occasionally, and then with great discomfort. So bad had Miller's physical problem become that in 1988 he was unable to defend his AT&T Pebble Beach National Pro-Am title.

Miller would make up for that in a most fascinating and sentimental way. From 1990–93, Miller had entered only six tournaments, and in 1994 he signed up for the AT&T if only for old times' sake; he loved playing on the Monterey Peninsula, had

With his son, Johnny Jr., as his caddie, Miller competes in the 1994 Masters. Injuries, business interests, and family commitments pulled Miller away from a regular Tour schedule.

won the event twice, and wanted to give his older sons, who had high golfing aspirations, a chance to compete on this level. But it was Dad who took the limelight. He shot a third-round 67 to move one stroke out of the lead with a round to play. And although he struggled in the final round under difficult weather conditions, his 74 at Pebble Beach was good enough to win by a stroke. If it is the last of Miller's victories, it was a beautiful way to go out.

Miller began doing color commentary of golf tournaments for NBC in the late 1980s, and almost immediately he became a highly popular, albeit sometimes controversial, figure. In his analyses of golf technique, he surprised many with how much he understood about the mechanics of the swing. He also proved to be quite candid in respect to players dealing with tournament pressure. Either way, he was a very articulate and insightful commentator.

Old Tom and Young Tom Morris

No father-son tandem has ever matched Tom Morris Sr. and Jr., who each won four British Opens in the early days of competitive golf. Old Tom is still the oldest ever British Open winner, at 46 in 1867, and Young Tom is the youngest, at 17 in 1868. The two finished 1–2 in the 1869 British Open, with Morris Jr. prevailing.

When Old Tom was young, he served as an apprentice clubmaker and ballmaker under Allan Robertson of St. Andrews, who was considered the best player of the day. The two formed a nearly unbeatable team in challenge matches against other Scottish duos. Morris, however, split with Robertson in business when Morris was quicker to accept the replacement of the old featherie ball with the gutta percha. In 1851, Morris left St. Andrews to become the custodian of the new links at Prestwick (Young Tom was born that year).

In 1860, the Open Championship was begun to determine Scotland's best golfer. Old Tom was runner-up to Willie Park in the first Open, then won in 1861, '62, '64, and '67. Morris Sr. returned to St. Andrews as pro and greenkeeper in 1865 and remained there until his death in 1908.

Young Tom, considered the most powerful player of the time, took the mantle from his father, winning the Open in 1868, '69, and '70, shooting a thenphenomenal 149 for 36 holes at Prestwick to win by 12 strokes the latter year. Young Tom's third straight victory gave him permanent possession of the champion's belt, and there was no competition in 1871. The next year, when the tournament resumed with a trophy as the prize (the same one awarded today), Young Tom won for the fourth straight time.

Morris Jr. finished third and second in the Open in the next two years. In 1875, his wife died during childbirth and the baby also did not survive. Young Tom never recovered from the shock, and he died three months later at age 24.

Above: *Old Tom Morris lived to be 86, spending his latter years as pro and greenkeeper at fabled St. Andrews.* Opposite page: *The younger Morris died at age 24, leaving a legacy that included three British Open championships before his 20th birthday.*

Byron Nelson

Many performance records are set in sports, and all are almost invariably broken. One, however, may well stand the test of time. That is Byron Nelson's streak of 11 consecutive victories on the PGA Tour, in 1945. The skein may never be topped not only because of its immensity, but because it would take a golfer who could play better than Nelson. There have been a few as good—Jones, Hogan, Snead, Nicklaus—but no one any better. The streak was the work of an all-time master golfer.

John Byron Nelson Jr. was born in Fort Worth, Texas, in 1912. He was one of three children of a grain and feed merchant, and he grew up in a house beside the Glen Garden Country Club, where Byron began caddying at age 10. A fellow caddie, born the same year, was Ben Hogan.

In his first caddie tournament, Nelson shot 118 "not counting the whiffs," as Byron recalled. The next year, he shot 79. "I just fell into it," said Byron when asked how he got so good so fast. He was also the recipient of sound instruction early on

Above: *Nelson's streak of 11 consecutive victories overshadowed his success in the majors. Here he sizes up a putt during a winning effort at the 1937 Masters. Opposite page: Nelson also won the 1940 PGA Championship.*

from the club pro, Ted Longworth, and his assistants, Dick and Jack Grout. The latter would be Jack Nicklaus's lifelong golf mentor.

In 1930, Nelson won his first important tournament, the Southwest Amateur. But he "came up" in the heart of the Depression, and he couldn't afford to play amateur golf. In the casual manner of the day, he turned pro in 1932. "Ted Longworth started a tourna-

During his brilliant winning streak, Nelson played 38 rounds of straight stroke play at 113-under-par, averaging 67.92 strokes per round.

ment in Texarkana, where he was now the pro," Nelson recalled. "The total prize money was $500, and there are people playing in it like Dick Metz and Ky Laffoon—established players—but I rode a bus over there carrying my little Sunday bag and suitcase, paid my $5 entry fee, and played in my first tournament as a pro. All you had to do then was say you were playing pro, and that was it."

Nelson finished third, won $75, and was encouraged. But he soon found himself struggling to make a living and took a job as professional at a golf club in Texarkana. He lived in a boarding house, saved his money, and practiced. "Very seldom did anybody come to the club before noon on any day," he said. "There was an excellent practice field, so I hit balls. I hit 'em down, then hit 'em back. So I got better and better."

He made a couple of forays on the pro Tour in 1933 and 1934, driving a Model-A Ford roadster. The first time out, he came back nearly broke. In '34, he did a bit better, but when offered a job as assistant pro at a fine club in New Jersey, he decided to take it. At about that time, steel shafts had taken over from hickory, and Nelson found he had to make major changes in his technique to adapt to them. He is credited as being the first important golfer to design a golf swing specifically for steel shafts: a more vertical action that, with irons especially, produced crisper, more accurate shots.

In 1936, Nelson won the Metropolitan Open, a PGA sectional (New York-New Jersey) event but one in which such golfing luminaries as Craig Wood, Paul Runyan, and Tommy

Armour—also club pros in the area—competed. It was the equivalent of a full-fledged PGA Tour event. Nelson was on his way.

In 1937, Nelson won the Masters, and in doing so gave first evidence of his proclivity for streaks of hot golf. With seven holes to play and four shots behind the leader, Nelson birdied the par-3 12th, eagled the par-5 13th, and parred in to pass Ralph Guldahl. (When he won the 1945 PGA Championship, during his fabled "streak," Nelson was two down with four holes to play in his second-round match against Mike Turnesa. He birdied the 33rd and 34th holes, eagled the 35th, and won, 1-up.)

After his '37 Masters victory, Nelson was chosen to play on that year's U.S. Ryder Cup team, indicating he was now one of the game's "establishment" players. He secured that place all the more in 1939 when he won the prestigious North and South Open, the Western Open, and the U.S. Open. In the latter, he hit one of the most memorable shots in golf history. In the final playoff round, on the long par-4 4th, Nelson drilled a 1-iron second shot into the hole for an eagle-2. A stunning shot, it reflected one of Nelson's greatest attributes as a golfer—phenomenal accuracy.

In 1940, Nelson won three tournaments. One was his third major, the PGA Championship, in which he was

Nelson greets heavyweight champion Joe Louis, an avid golfer, at the 1943 Tam O'Shanter All-America Amateur tournament in Chicago. Louis failed to qualify, but his presence helped raise money for the War Fund.

one down to Sam Snead with three holes to play in the final and birdied two of the last three to win, 1-up. From 1941–44, Nelson won 14 tournaments (eight of them in '44), including another Masters. Then came The Streak.

Nelson was rejected from military service during World War II owing to a blood deficiency, and it has been said that his run of victories in 1945 was not against the toughest possible fields. Hogan and Jimmy Demaret, in the Navy at the time, played in only two

Sports writer Herbert Warren Wind described Nelson as "a deeply pleasant and mild man…the first of our golfers whose technique was so grooved and compact that everyone referred to him as a machine."

of the "streak" events. However, Snead had been discharged from the Navy with a back problem, and he played in all but three of them.

In any case, stroke-play golf is essentially played against the course, and Nelson played them awfully well. During The Streak, he played 38 rounds of stroke play (we omit the first victory, a four-ball in which he had a partner, as well as the match-play formatted PGA Championship), which included two 18-hole playoff rounds against Snead to decide the Charlotte Open. Throughout The Streak, Nelson went round in 2,581 strokes for an average of 67.92 per round. In those 38 rounds, he was 113-under-par. Highlights? Nelson won the Iron Lung Open with a score of 263, a Tour record for 72 holes. In winning the Philadelphia Inquirer Invitational, he birdied five of the last six holes to win by a stroke.

Another demur regarding The Streak has been that Nelson had the advantage of preferred lies in the fairways at a few events, because not all the courses were in the best condition owing to shortages of machinery and materials during the war years. However, he also had to putt on greens that contrasted to those on the modern-day Tour; it's like comparing two-lane country roads to a new interstate highway. What's more, as Nelson once remarked, "back then you couldn't repair pitch marks or clean your ball on the greens."

There is simply no getting around it. Nelson's streak was an unmatchable exhibition of sustained excellence. Ironically, The Streak was ended when an amateur, Freddie Haas Jr., won the Memphis Invitational. But the next week, Nelson won again, then six more times for a total of 18 victories on the year, which itself is a record that still holds and may well hold as long as the 11 in a row.

Exhausted by his efforts, Nelson said after the '45 season that he was retiring from competitive golf. However, before making it final, he won six times in 1946 and won his last tournament in 1951, when he was 39. He then became an important teacher in the careers of Ken Venturi and Tom Watson, to name but two of his students, then a golf television analyst for many years. And beyond that, he was a warm, unpretentious ambassador for the game.

Because he played his best before the PGA Tour had become as popular as it would, and before television began extensive coverage of it, Nelson's talent at golf was not exposed as widely as was that of his contemporaries, Hogan and Snead, who were born in the same year. But those who were there knew what Nelson had. Everything.

Nelson was renowned for his accuracy, so the sight of "Lord Byron" mired in a bunker was unusual. "The only time Byron Nelson left the fairway," joked rival Jackie Burke, "was to pee in the bushes."

Jack Nicklaus

Jack Nicklaus experienced a rather cruel and unfair welcome to the major-league golf scene. How he handled it indicated that this was a man of great self-control and confidence, and one that had the instincts of a gentleman. All of these traits would become implicit as time went on, as Nicklaus would become one of the most dominant golfers in the history of the game.

When Jack Nicklaus won the 1962 U.S. Open, at historic Oakmont C.C. near Pittsburgh, it was his first victory as a professional. However, this superb achievement was clouded by the fact that he defeated Arnold Palmer in a playoff for the title. Palmer was at the height of his game and seemingly invincible as a player, and with his common-man, boy-next-door manner, he had reached an incredible popularity among the golfing public. Nicklaus, on the other hand, was rather overweight and had the air of a pampered country club golfer. Indeed, as everyone knew, he did grow up in a private club setting.

Thus, when he defeated Palmer rather handily in the playoff, not only outplaying but outhitting Palmer off the tee, he was treated with disdain. How dare he do this to "our Arnie?" Nicklaus suffered many sly indignities from galleries as well as some outwardly rude references to his weight. But through it all, Nicklaus never complained about the treatment. He took it in stride. As he did in his golf, he wore everyone down and brought everyone to his side with his consistently outstanding golf and superb sportsmanship. He was a champion in every way.

When Nicklaus romped to victory at the 1965 Masters, Bobby Jones remarked that Nicklaus was playing a game "with which I am not familiar." Jones was no doubt referring to the height of Nicklaus's shots with the long irons, which in fact enthralled everyone. They had an unusually high trajectory, the balls seeming to hang forever in the air before landing softly. They also carried astonishingly in their distance. But Jones, a most astute as well as articulate observer of a game he himself had mastered like few others, also had in mind Nicklaus's exceptional putting touch on fast greens as well as a level of poise under pressure that was incredible for so young a man. What would make all these attributes all the more exceptional was the length of time that they persisted.

Jack William Nicklaus was born in 1940 in Columbus, Ohio, the son of a pharmacist who at one time owned a small chain of local drugstores. Young Jack had good genes for athletics, as his father had been a fine athlete in a number of games. Jack

Above: His great rival, Arnold Palmer, slips the green jacket on Nicklaus after Jack's runaway victory at the 1965 Masters. Right: Nicklaus shows his emotions after narrowly missing a shot from the bunker during the 1968 U.S. Open. He finished second to Lee Trevino.

got quality instruction from the very start. His teacher was Jack Grout, who had been a fine player and became an even finer instructor. And he learned to play on one of golf's better championship layouts, the Donald Ross-designed Scioto C.C., where the Nicklauses were members.

Nicklaus showed he had the stuff of great golf almost from the day he took up the game, at age 10. Three years later, he shot a 3-under-par 69 at Scioto. It only got better. Much better. Nicklaus won five consecutive Ohio State Junior championships, beginning at age 12, and when he won the 1959 U.S. Amateur, he was at 19 years and eight months the youngest winner of the championship in 50 years. The '59 Amateur came down

to the last (36th) hole of the final. Nicklaus needed a nine-footer to close out 35-year-old Charlie Coe, who had twice won the title. He drilled it into the center of the cup. For all his prodigious length off the tee, that kind of clutch putting within the 15-foot range (and sometimes much longer) was perhaps the most distinguished characteristic of his game throughout all his competitive years.

While a student at Ohio State University, and No. 1 on the golf team, Nicklaus won another U.S. Amateur, in 1961. That year he also won the NCAA Championship, the Western Amateur, and the Big Ten championships; played Walker Cup golf; and finished fourth in the U.S. Open. Having conquered the amateur golf world, he turned professional.

His first outing as a regular on the PGA Tour, the Los Angeles Open in January 1962, was in retrospect curiously inauspicious. He finished well down the list and won less than $100. He continued to struggle through the winter while getting used to the travel—a new town and bed every week, restaurant food daily—and playing on the heavily trafficked public-fee courses that were not in the kind of condition to which he had become accustomed. On the other hand, he finished in the money in all 26 events entered and eventually won three times, including his historic U.S. Open. From that point on, he would set competitive records that may well never be matched.

In the next 25 years, Nicklaus won 67 more tournaments on the PGA Tour (including six Masters, four U.S. Opens, and five PGA Championships) and 18 abroad (including

Though sometimes wild off the tee, Nicklaus has a knack for escaping trouble. "There is only one man in history who could think and play golf at the same time," said Fulton Allem. "Jack Nicklaus."

three British Opens). His 20 major titles, including the two U.S. Amateur titles, are seven more than anyone else. Even the greatest of athletes do not win every competition they enter, and in golf that is especially the case. The next and perhaps more meaningful measure, then, of a player's talent is how close he has come to winning those times in which he doesn't in fact walk away with the victory. In this, Nicklaus is far and away the champion of champions. From 1962–69 on the PGA Tour alone, he finished in the top 10 in 122 out of 186 events entered and was second 24 times. From 1970–79, he was in the top 10 in 111 of 171 events and was second 20 times.

To refine this aspect of his record even more, from 1962–79—in a total of 335 PGA Tour events—Nicklaus missed the cut a mere nine times. More to the point, in the major championships in which he made the cut from 1962–79, Nicklaus's average finishes were sixth in the Masters, 11th in the U.S. Open, fifth in the British Open, and eighth in the PGA.

Of course, Nicklaus set many scoring records along the way. His 271 at the 1965 Masters smashed Ben Hogan's tourney record by three shots, and Jack won the tournament by nine. At the 1967 U.S. Open, Nicklaus drained a 22-foot birdie putt on the 72nd hole to break Hogan's Open record. The 275 mark stood until 1980, when Nicklaus, age 40, shot a 272. Jack's greatest year was 1972, when he prevailed in the Masters, U.S. Open, and five other Tour events; he lost the British Open by a stroke.

The years 1962–79 were essentially Nicklaus's prime years, but he would retain his incredible competitiveness beyond the time when most athletes, great or otherwise, are contenders. He had been the youngest to ever win the Masters, and in 1986 he became the oldest winner of that title (at

Nicklaus has maintained an extraordinary level of play for the better part of four decades. "He's been on a 30-year lucky streak," joked Frank Beard, when asked if Nicklaus is really that good.

46), which he won with great flair. In the final 10 holes, the old man recorded six birdies and an eagle.

Playing a limited number of events on the Senior PGA Tour, Nicklaus won 10 times (out of 32 tries) from 1990–95, twice winning the U.S. Senior Open. And in 1996, playing in his 40th consecutive U.S. Open—itself a record—on the monstrous Oakland Hills C.C. course, Nicklaus finished in a tie for 27th with the same score (287) that Hogan made to win the Open on the same layout. When he strode up the 18th fairway to conclude his play, Nicklaus was greeted with a thunderously warm ovation.

Nicklaus has "officially" and unofficially been dubbed the greatest golfer in the history of the game. Based on his record, and with longevity a definite part of the equation, the designation can hardly be denied.

One of the most beloved figures in American sports, Nicklaus marches on. "It's like having a freezer full of ice cream," he said of his thirst for competition. "When you come down to the last bite, you want more."

Greg Norman

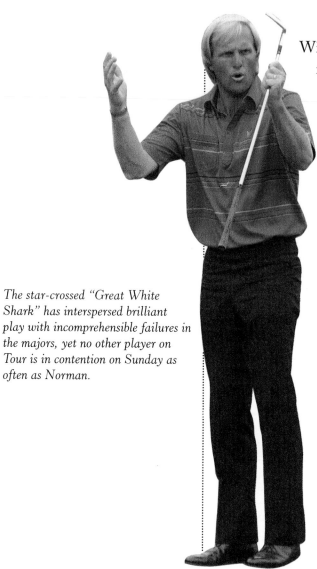

Throughout his career, Greg Norman has been an enigma. Winner of about 70 tournaments worldwide and over $10 million in prize money on the U.S. PGA Tour alone, Norman still may go down in the game's annals for how many major championships he lost—more specifically, how he lost them.

In 1986 alone, Norman held the lead in all four of the majors going into the final round of play, yet he won only one of them, the British Open. He is also the only golfer in history to have lost a playoff for each of the majors ('84 U.S. Open, '87 Masters, '89 British Open, '93 PGA). In the 1996 Masters, his collapse in the final round was one of the most astonishing and perplexing of them all. He shot a course record-tying 63 in the first round, then—with a six-shot lead going into the final round—shot a 78 to finish second, five shots behind the winner, Nick Faldo. It was the largest lead ever "blown" in the last round of a major championship. Yes, it's been a star-crossed career for Norman, full of amazing highs and equally amazing lows.

Born in the mining town of Mount Isa in Queensland, Australia, in 1955, Gregory John Norman was by his own description a "skinny, scrawny" youth. Self-conscious of his physique and bound to overcome it, his first athletic interests were in the contact games—rugby, Australian rules football, cricket, squash, and particularly swimming and surfing. He also worked diligently at weight lifting to develop his body. He did indeed become an impressive physical specimen—just over six feet tall, weighing 180 pounds, with broad shoulders, a trim waist, and strong legs. He developed an aggressive, power-oriented golf game that would be adored by the golfing public.

The star-crossed "Great White Shark" has interspersed brilliant play with incomprehensible failures in the majors, yet no other player on Tour is in contention on Sunday as often as Norman.

After his Masters collapse in 1996, Norman had only one victory to show for the eight majors in which he had taken a lead into the final round. He emerged victorious at the 1993 British Open, after which Norman said, "I'm not a person who boasts, but I'm just in awe of the way I hit the golf ball today."

Norman did not take up golf until he was 16. His father, a mining engineer, did not play much, but Norman's mother was a three-handicap golfer. While caddying for his mother, Norman decided to hit a few to see what it was like. He was a long-ball hitter from the start, and with that as the carrot he took up the game. Within two years, he went from a 27 handicap to a scratch golfer, and he became a significant factor in Australian amateur golf. He turned pro in 1976 and began competing on the Australian Tour. He then spread his wings to play the international circuits.

From 1977–82, "The Shark" won at least one tournament every year, including such prestigious titles as the Australian Open, Australian Masters, French Open, and Dunlop Masters. In his first U.S. Masters, in 1981, he finished a very respectable fourth, only three shots off Tom Watson's winning score and one behind runners-up Jack Nicklaus and Johnny Miller.

In 1984, Norman began spending more time on the U.S. PGA Tour, where that year he won the Kemper and Canadian Opens. He also was in a playoff for the U.S. Open, where he exhibited for the first time a tendency to self-destruct under ultimate pressure. Three shots behind Fuzzy Zoeller with nine holes to play, Norman drew even after 17 holes and then drove well on the 18th. However,

Norman's victory in The Players Championship was the highlight of a 1994 season that saw him average 68.81 strokes per round en route to his third Vardon Trophy.

his 6-iron approach was pushed some 40 yards right of the green into a grandstand. After a free drop, he managed to save his par (4) with an incredible 45-foot putt over severely undulating terrain. In the playoff, though, he was overwhelmed, 67–75.

In the 1986 Masters, Norman's proclivity to fail at the moment of truth reared up again. Needing a par-4 on the last hole to tie Nicklaus, he hit a 4-iron approach far right of the green and bogied the hole to finish tied for second. Three months later, he won his first major, the British Open, by five strokes. But the following month, he let Bob Tway back into the PGA Championship, shooting a final-round 76 to give up a four-shot lead with 18 to play and setting the stage for Tway's smashing finish; he holed a bunker shot on the 72nd hole to win, by two.

The pattern was settling in. Norman would either win big, dominating the field, or more often than not let others catch him with his mediocre to poor play against an opponent's fine play and occasional spectacular single shot. He lost the 1987 Masters when Larry Mize holed a 45-yard chip shot in sudden death.

Through all the shocking defeats and collapses, even as he has cut back his overly aggressive game management, Norman has maintained a calm public demeanor. He simply points to his overall record, which is indeed remarkable. Over 14 seasons through 1996 on the U.S. Tour, he posted more than 100 top-10 finishes, including 17 victories, and won the Vardon Trophy for low scoring average three times. The game is there, and of course the money has followed. In 1995 alone, he set a PGA Tour season record for

Left and below: Unlike his critics, Norman accentuates the positive. "I'll win here," he vowed at Augusta National after the 1996 Masters. "I will. Something great is waiting for me down the line in golf. I don't know what it is, but I have to believe that. If I don't, hell, I might as well put my clubs away for good."

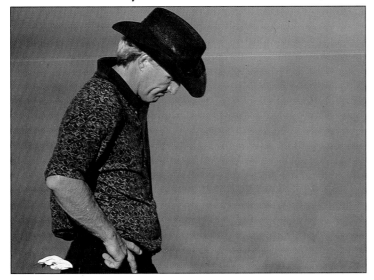

money won with $1,654,959. He soared to No. 1 on the career money list despite playing a limited schedule.

And yet, he is found wanting. A golfer of his ability is supposed to win more majors, and certainly more than a few of those he leads going into the last round of play. He shrugs at the notion and says he will just keep trying. Of that, we can be sure.

*Ouimet (center) parlayed a home-course advantage
into a shocking upset of British professionals Harry
Vardon (left) and Ted Ray (right) in the 1913 U.S.
Open at The Country Club in Brookline, Massachusetts.
It was Ouimet's first appearance in the Open.*

GOLF LEGENDS OF ALL TIME

Francis Ouimet

*F*rancis Ouimet wasn't a completely untried and unknown golfer when he achieved his monumental U.S. Open victory in 1913. The 20-year-old Boston boy was the current amateur champion in Massachusetts, a state with some of the game's best players at the time, and two weeks earlier had reached the second round of the U.S. Amateur championship before losing to the eventual winner. Still, for Ouimet it was like coming out of nowhere to win a playoff over Harry Vardon and Ted Ray.

There was enough wonderful coincidence in Ouimet's victory to fill a romantic heart to the fullest. Ouimet grew up a pitch-shot distance from the site of his achievement, The Country Club in Brookline, Massachusetts, where he began his golf career as a caddie. He was a modest, polite, tallish young man with a studious air. And, perhaps most significant of all, he was an amateur who not only beat the two of the best players in golf in a head-to-head contest, but they were professionals to boot. In those years, amateurism was far more highly regarded.

Professional golfers were considered mere mercenaries who were treated not unlike second-class citizens; for instance, they were not allowed into the clubhouses of private clubs. And, of course, Ouimet was an American defeating the lords of *British golf,* at a time when the Boston Tea Party that took place only a few miles away and was so important to the American Revolution was still fresh in the national psyche. Ouimet was the first amateur to win the U.S. Open and only the second native-born

The 1913 U.S. Open was a celebration of youth. The fresh-faced Ouimet was only 20 years old when he won the championship, and his caddie, Eddie Lowery, was only 10.

Ouimet (right) helped popularize golf in America, expanding the stage for the likes of Bobby Jones (left). They are shown together in 1930, the year Jones won the Grand Slam.

American to do so. The positive repercussions of Ouimet's victory could never be measured precisely, but there is little doubt that it led to a far wider interest in golf in the United States.

Ouimet was not a fluke. In winning the 1913 Open, he staged a rally in the fourth round to force an 18-hole playoff. He dominated in the extra round, posting a 72 to Vardon's 77 and Ray's 78. In 1914, Ouimet opened his defense of the U.S. Open crown with a 69, only one shot back of the leader and eventual winner, Walter Hagen. Ouimet ended up tied for fifth. Two weeks later, Francis won the U.S. Amateur championship, trouncing by a whopping 6 & 5 margin the man who had defeated him the year before in that event, four-time champion Jerry Travers.

A serious student of swing technique, and an early investigator of the mental side of golf, Ouimet continued to play at a high level for some 20 years. In 1920, he won the North and South Amateur, a championship that was a close second to the U.S. Amateur in prestige. That same year, he went to the finals of the U.S. Amateur, defeating Bobby Jones in the semifinals before losing to Chick Evans. Evidence that he had crafted a long-term golf game, Ouimet in 1925 made a spirited try for the U.S. Open, finishing only one stroke off the winning total posted by Jones and Willie Macfarlane. Then in 1931, 17 years after his U.S. Open triumph, he won his second U.S. Amateur, defeating Jack Westland in the final by 6 & 5.

It was not quite his last hurrah. The next year in the Amateur, Ouimet shot a 30 on the first nine of his first match and went to the semifinals before losing to a future U.S. Open champion, Johnny Goodman. Ouimet would play on the first nine U.S. Walker Cup teams (beginning with 1922's unofficial meeting through 1934), was the playing captain on the last two teams, and was nonplaying captain four times afterwards.

Ouimet was also the catalyst for what became a more progressive reading of the Amateur Code. In 1916, Ouimet was banned from amateur competition because of an interest he had in a sporting goods store in Boston. The USGA apparently felt he was cashing in on his celebrity status as a golfer. Nothing could be farther from the truth. Ouimet was a devoted advocate of amateur golf, and he had spurned opportunities to truly cash in by playing exhibitions for money and endorsing products. The ban caused an angry furor for what was deemed a too-narrow amateur status stance, and also because the soft-spoken, affable Ouimet was much loved by the golfing public. The USGA more or less sideslipped the controversy in 1918, after he was inducted into the U.S. Army. The USGA used this event to lift the ban and reinstate Ouimet's amateur status.

Not one to hold a grudge, Ouimet would later serve for many years on the USGA's Executive Committee. In time, the USGA, with some input from Ouimet, would soften its Amateur Code. Such was the esteem in which Ouimet was held in the world of golf that, in 1951, he became the first American to be honored as the captain of the Royal & Ancient Golf Club of St. Andrews, Scotland. He died in 1967.

Ouimet devoted a lifetime to golf and was one of its leading dignitaries. Long past his prime here, he tees off at the 1941 Masters. Ten years later, he became the first American to be named captain of the Royal & Ancient Golf Club of St. Andrews.

Arnold Palmer

*I*t is the rare athlete who achieves a level of popularity that transcends his sport and becomes a national folk hero. Such was the case with Arnold Palmer. His rise to such heights was the result of a unique combination of elements. When Palmer won the 1960 U.S. Open, with an exhilarating final-round 65, the national network telecasting of golf was just beginning to take hold. The conclusion of his great round was seen by millions, who also saw in the author of that remarkable finish a refreshingly animated athlete responding with an obvious, visor-tossing exhilaration that golf fans had not seen before.

What's more, the way Palmer played the game had an endearing quality with which the mass of average golfers could identify. He swung hard and fast and had a less than classic, gyrating follow-through. He hit the ball with great authority and for distance, and he did not play with the stolid caution of golfers past. Palmer took chances, "went for broke," and the crowd loved him for it. They created what came to be called "Arnie's Army," loyal followers who chased after and cheered him through his prime and even after he was well past his most effective years as a competitive golfer.

Had Palmer not also been a winner, all his charismatic charm would have been little more than an interesting sidebar to golf. But he was a winner, a big winner. By 1960, Palmer had already won 13 tournaments on the PGA Tour, including

Opposite page and below: Palmer has had a lifelong love affair with golf, as evidenced by the joy with which he plays the game. "What other people find in poetry or art museums," he once said, "I find in the flight of a good drive."

the first of the four Masters he would capture. The '60 Open victory at Cherry Hills C.C. in Denver had the stuff of which legends are made.

The final round was played on Saturday afternoon. During lunch, Palmer asked companions, "I may shoot 65. What would that do?" "Nothing," said golf writer Bob Drum. "You're too far back." "The hell I am," Palmer snapped. "A 65 would give me 280, and 280 wins Opens."

Three times Palmer had tried to drive the 1st green, and three times he had failed. That afternoon, Palmer went for it again. He hit a smoking tee shot, his ball bounded through a belt of rough fronting the green, and it rolled onto the putting surface 20 feet from the hole. It was a 346-yard clout. He birdied that hole, and five more on the front side, to turn in 30, and a hero was born for the ages.

Palmer strikes a shot at the 1954 U.S. Amateur, where he achieved his first significant victory. He turned pro later that year and went on to capture 60 victories on the PGA Tour.

Earlier in that same monumental season, Palmer had won his second Masters. When he entered the British Open, the world of golf was excited by the possibility of the first modern-day Grand Slam—victories in the four major championships (the PGA would be the fourth leg). He came up one shot shy of the winner at St. Andrews, Kel Nagle, but in merely going to the British Open he revived interest in the grand, old event, an interest that had flagged in previous years because the dominant American stars regularly bypassed it. With the game's history in mind, Palmer conscientiously sought to bring the British Open back to its rightful place in golf. He did

Arnie towels off after the final round of the 1961 Masters was postponed because of rain. When play resumed the next day, Palmer erased Gary Player's four-stroke lead—only to double-bogey the 18th hole and lose by one stroke.

that, by dint of his play and his personal appeal, and the game should be eternally grateful to Palmer for this one of his many contributions to it.

Arnold Daniel Palmer was born in 1929 in Latrobe, Pennsylvania. His father, known as "Deke," was the greenkeeper at Latrobe C.C. and later became its head professional. A good golfer himself—although lame in one leg from having polio as a youth—the elder Palmer was a hard-driving man who demanded the best from his only son, whom he taught to play when Arnold was three years old. The lesson was simple: Eschew "classic" form if it didn't come naturally. Take the club back slowly and then hit the ball as hard as you can. There were times in his career when Palmer considered altering his swing to make it more fluid and graceful, but he would inevitably go back to his roots and rock and sock it even when it seemed to cost him victories.

For example, Palmer's bold style of play was counted as the reason he lost the 1966 U.S. Open, at the Olympic Club in San Francisco. Palmer had a seven-shot lead over Billy Casper with only nine holes to play. Rather than play carefully and nurse his huge lead, he continued to fire away, because that was his way and also because his mind was on breaking the U.S. Open record score of 276. He needed to par the last six holes to do that, but he instead went 6-over to finish in a tie with Casper. He lost in the playoff, again after building up a substantial lead early but giving it up with his slash-and-burn style of golf. But Palmer's golf swing and how he used it reflected his true daredevil character, which is why he was so admired by golf fans, win or lose.

Palmer played some amateur golf prior to turning pro, and he showed promise. He entered Wake Forest University on a golf scholarship

arranged by his best friend, Buddy Worsham, younger brother of the 1947 U.S. Open champion. Arnie won the Southern Intercollegiate title in 1950, twice went to the semifinals of the prestigious North and South Amateur, and won the celebrated All-American Amateur at Chicago's Tam O'Shanter C.C. by nine shots over the formidable Frank Stranahan.

But Palmer's ascent in golf was slowed by the tragic death of his friend Worsham, who was killed in a car accident. Palmer dropped out of school, joined the Coast Guard, and when discharged took a job as a paint salesman. He did keep up his golf, though, and—once past the pain of Worsham's death—got back in gear. In 1954, Palmer won the U.S. Amateur championship at the Country Club

Above and right: Palmer, wrote Peter Alliss, "brought excitement to golf and the TV ratings for golf soared. In tournaments, though many might have followed their own favorites, Palmer always had his 'Army' and still has today. In the States, he made the greatest contribution to the popularizing of golf since Walter Hagen."

of Detroit. He would always say that this was the toughest victory of his career, owing to the match-play format. Later that year, Palmer turned professional with the intention of playing the tournament circuit. He never did hold a club job, but he did come to own the golf club where he grew up as well as the Bay Hill Golf Club in Orlando, where he annually hosts the PGA Tour's Nestle Invitational.

Through 1996, Palmer ranked fourth in the PGA Tour's record book for total number of victories with 60. His four Masters came every other year from 1958–64, and all were won in grand fashion. In 1958, Palmer eagled the 67th hole to give him the edge he needed. In 1960, he birdied the last two holes to edge Ken Venturi by a stroke. In '62, he fired a sizzling 31 on the back nine of a playoff to win by three. And in '64, he romped to a six-shot victory.

Palmer's most productive stretch of winning golf came from 1960–63, when he won 29 tournaments. He also won 19 international events, including two British Opens (1961 and '62), and 10 Senior PGA Tour tournaments, including the U.S. Senior Open (1981). He is tied with Jack Nicklaus for the most consecutive years winning at least one tournament (17), and he was the first golfer to reach the $1 million mark in career prize money. Palmer also holds the record for most Ryder Cup Match victories with 22. He played on six U.S. Ryder Cup teams and was twice the captain.

Moreover, with his trim waist, muscular arms and upper body, and power-game style, Palmer changed the perception nongolfers somehow had of the game—that it was not athletic. That, along with his ready smile, an unpretentious manner that projected easy access by the gallery (he became known for never passing up an autograph request), and a readiness to talk openly with the press whenever asked, would make Arnold Palmer a household name—golf households and otherwise.

Betrayed by his putter in the twilight of his career, Palmer battled on. "There are very few truths in putting," he said. "You get the ball in the hole, and it doesn't matter how."

Henry Picard

He was one of the best players in the game during the 1930s, but Henry Picard is also remembered for his generosity. In 1937, Picard gave a driver to a young Sam Snead, telling him the one he was using wasn't suited to his game. Snead credited it with turning his game around and used the club for more than 20 years. Picard also offered financial assistance to Ben Hogan when Hogan was down to nearly his last dollar. Hogan later dedicated a book to Picard.

Picard was born in Massachusetts in 1907 and moved to South Carolina when he was 17. He scored his first Tour victory in 1932 and another two years later. Then his game blossomed. Picard won five tournaments in 1935 and led the Masters by four strokes after two rounds before fading to fourth place.

Three more victories followed in 1936 and four in 1937. His two wins in 1938 included one at the Masters, where Picard beat Harry Cooper and Ralph Guldahl by two strokes. Picard's best year came in 1939, when he won eight tournaments and was the Tour's leading money winner.

Picard won the 1939 PGA Championship in dramatic fashion over Byron Nelson. Henry was 1 down going to the 36th hole, where both players nearly drove the green on a short par-4. Nelson chipped to 12 feet and then missed, and Picard made his birdie from four feet to square the match. On the first extra hole, Picard hit his drive under a truck. After getting relief, Picard hit his approach shot to seven feet. He made the birdie putt and won the championship when Nelson missed a birdie try from five feet.

Picard had one of the best swings of his day and was a fine long-iron player. He finished his career with 26 Tour victories, 20 of them coming from 1935–39. He tired of competition after that, cutting back his schedule starting in 1940 even though he was still playing well. He settled into the life of a club professional and respected instructor, scoring his last Tour win in 1945.

Right and opposite page: *The dapper Picard played brilliantly in 1939, defeating Byron Nelson in the PGA Championship, winning seven other tournaments, and finishing as the year's leading money winner with $10,303. He also found time to work on young Ben Hogan's grip and swing.*

Gary Player

If nothing else, Gary Player could have gone down in golf history as the most widely traveled champion of all time. However, it is generally agreed that even if he didn't have to put a million or so miles on his personal odometer, he would still have had his extraordinary career in major-league competitive golf. All professional golfers, by definition, must play on the road. Player's globetrotting was just more extensive and gave his record a little different twist.

Gary Jim Player was born in 1935 in a suburb of Johannesburg, South Africa, but he was raised in that nation's capital. Despite being small and slight of build, he stood out in numerous "physical" sports—cricket, rugby, soccer, track, swimming, and diving—and even as an adult seemed no bigger than a jockey compared to almost all the golfers he outplayed in winning every major championship in the game at least once. He is one of only four to have done so, which puts him in the company of Ben Hogan, Jack Nicklaus, and Gene Sarazen.

Player took up golf at 15 at the behest of his father, himself a good player. He was hooked on the game from the start, a romance that may also have had to do with his meeting the girl who would become his wife. Her father, Jock Verwey, was a well-known golf professional in Johannesburg. Player would work for him as an assistant pro.

Opposite page and below: Player succeeded countryman Bobby Locke as South Africa's best player. After turning pro at age 18, he enjoyed immediate success, and at 23 he won the 1959 British Open at Muirfield. His nine victories in major championships are exceeded only by Jack Nicklaus, Bobby Jones, and Walter Hagen.

GOLF LEGENDS OF ALL TIME

Early on, Player had an unorthodox and rather bizarre golf swing, in large part the result of feeling that he had to hit the ball as hard as possible to make up for his size. Yet, he did well at the highest level, an indication of his innate talent at the game as well as a competitive zeal to sustain that talent. In 1956, he won his first South African Open (he would win 13 in all) as well as a tournament on the British Tour. He also finished fourth in the British Open that year.

Player then went about the process of altering his overly strong grip and long and complicated swing, and almost immediately he began his rise to the top of the heap. Interestingly, he did not lose any power. Pound for pound, he was one of the longest hitters in the game, and he was his own best example of the advice he has always given youngsters starting up in golf: First learn to hit the ball for distance, which will always stay with you, then learn to golf the ball for score.

Recognizing that the U.S. PGA Tour was the ultimate training (and proving) ground for big-time golf, Player in 1957 began traveling regularly to play in the United States. In 1958, he won his first American Tour event, the Kentucky Derby Open. In nine tournaments on the U.S. circuit that year, he finished in the top 10 10 times, including a second-place showing in the U.S. Open.

In 1959, Player won the first of the three British Opens he would capture. In 1961, he won three times on the U.S. Tour, including his first Masters to become the first foreign player to win that championship. In that Masters, a main feature of Player's golf would come to the fore. On the last day, playing to a delicate pin position from the greenside bunker on the 18th hole, he got down in two for a 280 total. A few minutes later, Arnold Palmer made a 6 from almost the identical spot in the same bunker to

At his peak, Player was considered one of the "Big Three" along with Jack Nicklaus and Arnold Palmer. Here he dons the green jacket after beating Palmer (back left) by one stroke to win the 1961 Masters.

finish in a tie for second. In practicing bunker shots, Player would often stay at it until he had holed at least one, sometimes more.

Player's reputation had now grown to such an extent that he, along with Palmer and Nicklaus, were considered golf's "Big Three." That was in part a bit of promotional wizardry by the agent handling all three players, but it was still pretty close to reality. From 1961–74, Player would win 17 times on the U.S. Tour, including one more PGA Championship ('72), two more Masters (1974 and '78), and a U.S. Open ('65). In all, he won 21 times on the U.S. circuit. He also won the Australian Open seven times and the World Match Play championship five times, and he was twice the individual winner of the World Cup. On the Senior PGA Tour, Player won 18 times from 1985–95, a tribute not only to the quality of the game he put together years earlier and with which he never stopped adapting, but to the superb physical condition that he always maintained.

Through much of Player's career, he was a red flag for people protesting, often quite vigorously, the infamous policy of apartheid that was long extant in his country. He invariably handled it with admirable diplomacy, and he made a point to invite such black golfers as Lee Elder to play at the South African PGA Championship and other tournaments in Player's homeland before the racial policy there was dissolved. In this, Player has contributed to golf in a way more valuable than his competitive record.

Above and right: *Fitness, practice, and positive thinking have been lifelong pursuits for Player. The "Man in Black" maintains his body in peak condition; abstains from alcohol, tobacco, coffee, tea, sugar, and fried foods; and works incessantly on his game.*

Nick Price

It took Nick Price a while to find the winning touch on the PGA Tour, but once he did he dominated like no one had since Tom Watson in his heyday. From 1992–94, Price won 11 PGA Tour events and five international titles for a total of 16 victories. Three of the victories came in major championships.

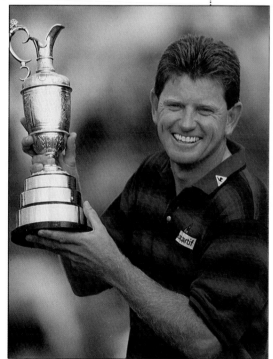

After finishing second at the British Open in 1982 and 1988, Price won the Claret Jug in 1994. He added five victories in the United States that year and topped the Tour money list.

Though Price turned out to be a late bloomer, for a while he looked like an early prodigy. The Zimbabwean won the Junior World in San Diego in 1974, claimed his first South African event at age 22 in 1979, and won in Europe the next year. At the 1982 British Open, he led on the final nine before playing the last six holes in 4-over-par to finish second to Watson. The next year, his first on the PGA Tour, he won the World Series of Golf.

Then, for the next eight years, Price went winless on the PGA Tour. He had five runner-up finishes and ranked between 22nd and 43rd on the money list every year from 1986–90, but he couldn't quite put everything together in one week. He finished second in the British Open again in 1988, this time falling to Seve Ballesteros's closing round of 65. Things finally changed in 1991 when Price won the GTE Byron Nelson Classic and Canadian Open. His confidence boosted, and putting better than he had in his life, Price was ready to go on a sustained roll.

He won twice in the U.S. in 1992, including his first major, the PGA Championship. Price had four PGA Tour wins in 1993—the Players Championship in March and three straight starts in the summer. He was even better in 1994, winning five times in just 19 events on the PGA Tour plus finally capturing the British Open. With his six-stroke romp in the PGA Championship, Price became the first player to win two straight majors since Watson in 1982. Price passed the $1 million mark in earnings in 1992, '93, and '94, leading the money list the latter two years. He won the Vardon Trophy in 1993.

In a strange day at the 1989 U.S. Open at Oak Hill, Price was one of four golfers to score a hole-in-one on the same hole. The odds of four pros acing the same hole on the same day were 8.7 million to one, according to the National Hole-in-One Association.

Betsy Rawls

Undoubtedly the best golfer in history to graduate from college Phi Beta Kappa with a degree in physics and math, Betsy Rawls won 55 events in her LPGA Tour career. Four of those came in the U.S. Women's Open, a record she shares with Mickey Wright.

Rawls started playing golf when she was 17. Four years later, in 1949, she won the first of two straight Texas Amateur titles. After completing her studies at the University of Texas, Rawls decided her future was in professional golf, even though the LPGA Tour was just getting off the ground and purses were low.

Rawls's first victory came in the 1951 U.S. Women's Open, where she finished five strokes ahead of Louise Suggs. Jackie Pung was the victim in both of Rawls's next two Women's Open victories. In 1953, Rawls won an 18-hole playoff, 71–77. Pung was an apparent winner in 1957, but she was disqualified for signing an incorrect scorecard, handing the victory to Rawls. Rawls won her fourth Open in 1960 thanks largely to a third-round 68, which tied the existing 18-hole record.

Rawls won four other major titles: the Western Open in 1952 and 1959 and the LPGA Championship in 1959 and 1969. She won at least one tournament in every year from 1951–65, and she claimed her last victory in 1972 at the age of 44. She won 10 events in 1959, a single-season total bettered by only Wright, and led the money list in 1952 and '59. She won the Vare Trophy in 1959.

Not an exceptionally long hitter, Rawls's strength was her touch around the greens. Her career victory total ranks fourth on the all-time LPGA list behind Wright, Kathy Whitworth, and Patty Berg.

After she retired from competition in 1975, Rawls became active in tournament administration. She was the LPGA's tournament director from 1976–81 and then became the executive director of the McDonald's Championship. In 1980, she became the first woman to serve on the rules committee for the men's U.S. Open.

Above: *While not a long hitter off the tee, Rawls was exceedingly accurate with her irons. Opposite page: A stunned Rawls reacts upon being awarded the 1957 U.S. Women's Open championship after the apparent winner, Jackie Pung, signed an incorrect scorecard.*

Chi Chi Rodriguez

Growing up in a poor family in Puerto Rico, Juan "Chi Chi" Rodriguez began his long road to golf fame and fortune at the age of nine by swinging at tin cans with a limb from a guava tree. Ed Dudley, the pro at the local course, gave Rodriguez a job as a shoeshine boy, then as caddie master, and fostered the enthusiastic youngster's development as a player. At 17, Rodriguez, who took his nickname from his favorite baseball player, finished second in the Puerto Rico Open. He then joined the U.S. Army and began saving money for a shot at the PGA Tour.

Rodriguez made it to the Tour in 1960, at age 24, and scored his first victory three years later. Though he stood 5'7" and weighed 130 pounds, Rodriguez took a ferocious swing and hit the ball reasonably far off the tee. He was also one of the game's finest shot-makers, able to work the ball left-to-right or right-to-left at will and to get out of trouble with a variety of imaginative shots.

Chi Chi also became known for entertaining the galleries with his quips and antics, which included putting his hat over the hole after making a putt and wielding his putter like a sword in celebration. He toned down his act slightly after a few leading pros persuaded him that it was sometimes distracting to fellow players, but he remained a fan favorite.

Rodriguez finished his Tour career with eight victories, enjoying his best year in 1964 when he had two wins and was ninth on the money list. He ranked among the top 50 money winners in every year but one from 1963–74.

Rodriguez's game blossomed on the Senior Tour, which he became eligible for late in 1985. He led the money list in 1987 when he won seven tournaments, including the PGA Seniors Championship, and finished in the top three 14 times. In his first six senior seasons, he won 20 times. Rodriguez is also known for his work for charitable causes, particularly the Chi Chi Rodriguez Youth Foundation.

Opposite page and below: *Chi Chi's lighthearted sword act tended to obscure his serious side. As a kid growing up in Puerto Rico, he vowed to rise from poverty to the heights of professional golf, but his friends, he said, "told me I was a hound dreaming about pork chops."*

Donald Ross

*L*ike many of his countrymen, Donald Ross emigrated from Scotland to the United States around the turn of the century to become a golf professional. His true talent, however, proved to be designing golf courses. Incredibly, Ross would design or improve more than 500 courses during a 45-year career.

Ross was born in 1873 in Dornoch, Scotland, home of the Royal Dornoch links that would influence his own style as an architect. The son of a stonemason, he worked as an apprentice under Old Tom Morris in St. Andrews, then became pro and greenkeeper at Royal Dornoch. He was influenced to come to America by Robert Wilson, a Harvard professor who spent summers in Dornoch.

Ross arrived in the U.S. in 1898 with, it is said, two dollars in his pocket. Wilson helped him land a job as pro at Oakley Country Club in Watertown, Massachusetts. Ross got an even bigger break shortly thereafter when he met James W. Tufts, whose family was building a new resort in Pinehurst, North Carolina. Ross signed on as the professional and quickly set about revising the first course there and designing a second one.

The Pinehurst No. 2 course, which would become his masterpiece, opened in 1903, and Ross continued to make changes on it until 1935. Ross's work at Pinehurst gained him a reputation as an architect, and his services were soon in demand as golf courses were sprouting up around the nation. By the 1920s, the golden age of architecture in the U.S., his company was working on dozens of projects at a time. Ross designed courses in 30 states, plus Canada and Cuba, though he remained affiliated with Pinehurst until his death in 1948. Ross's other famous courses include Seminole in Florida, Oakland Hills in Michigan, Oak Hill in New York, and Scioto and Inverness in Ohio. He is known for his natural use of the terrain and for crowned greens that offer subtle challenges on approach and pitch shots.

Right: Although he traveled far and wide as a player and course architect, Ross is remembered mostly for his association with Pinehurst Country Club in North Carolina, where he won the North and South Open in 1903, 1905, and 1906. Opposite page: Ross appears with Ben Hogan, who won the North and South in 1940 and 1942.

Paul Runyan

Standing just 5'7" and weighing about 125 pounds, Paul Runyan was known as "Little Poison" because of his deadly game on and around the greens. His short-game skills earned him a pair of PGA Championships and a total of 29 victories, most of them in the 1930s.

The son of an Arkansas farmer, Runyan did not consider himself a natural as a player, but through hard work he reached the point where he was ready to try the pro tour in 1930 at the age of 21. Runyan won twice that year and scored at least one victory in every year of the 1930s except for 1937. He was the best player in the game for a two-year stretch, winning nine tournaments in 1933 and seven in 1934 and leading the money list both years.

Both of Runyan's PGA Championship victories came in final matches against long hitters. In 1934, he beat Craig Wood in a tense 38-hole match by getting up and down on the last three holes. At the 36th hole, both players made 12-foot par putts. Wood reached the par-5 37th hole in two, but Runyan was able to chip close for a tying birdie. Finally, Runyan claimed the match on the 38th hole by pitching over a bunker to eight feet and sinking the winning par putt.

Runyan's 1938 win over Sam Snead was an 8 & 7 romp, the biggest margin of victory in a final in the 39 years the PGA Championship was held at match play. Snead outdrove him by 50 yards on nearly every hole, but Runyan was deadly accurate and played the 29 holes of the final in 6-under.

Though Runyan was only 30 when he beat Snead, he added only two more victories, the last in 1941, and virtually retired from competition after World War II. Runyan went on to become a respected teacher and a good senior player in the days before there was a Senior Tour, finishing second in the PGA Seniors Championship in 1959 and '60 and winning it in '61 and '62.

Opposite page and above: In 1934, the Tour's first official season, Runyan led the money list with $6,767. He had to win seven tournaments, including the PGA Championship, to reach that modest figure.

GOLF LEGENDS OF ALL TIME

Gene Sarazen

Opposite page and below: *Naturally curious, Sarazen proposed expanding the size of the cup from 4¼ inches to eight inches. Later in his career, he invented the sand wedge. On the course, he was bold, temperamental, and enthusiastic.*

A first-generation American and son of an immigrant Italian carpenter, Gene Sarazen, née Saraceni, was born in 1902 in Harrison, New York. Like all would-be golfers of the working class, Sarazen got into golf as a caddie, at the age of 10.

"I walked to the course where I caddied (Apawamis G.C.) and made up nine holes along the way in empty lots," he said. He played them on the way to the course, and on the way home. "But nobody gave me lessons," he said. "I used to watch the players in tournaments. My favorite was Walter Hagen. I admired his ways, his technique, the way he would slash at the ball. And the way he dressed. He was my hero."

At 14, Sarazen came down with empyema, a lung ailment, and nearly died. "I remember lying in the hospital and the priests coming in and pulling the curtain around me," he said. "They figured I was going to go, and were preparing the last rites. That was in 1916, and in 1920 I was still so weak I could hardly break 80."

Two years later, he won the New Orleans Open, his first professional victory, and then surprised everyone (but himself) by becoming the winner of the U.S. Open. He won the '22 Open with the kind of verve, nerve, and brass that characterized his personality and golf game for the next 30 years. Four shots off the lead with one round to play at the Skokie C.C., he caught fire. On the last hole, he was deep in contention and had a crucial decision to make.

"I hit a good drive," he said, "and for my second there was water to the left and out-of-bounds on the right. My caddie wanted me to play safe, but I heard somebody say [Bobby] Jones and [Bill] Mehlhorn [playing a few holes back] were doing well. So I said, 'Oh hell, give me that brassie.' I shot right for the green and put it about 12 feet from the cup. I made the putt for a birdie. On the 17th, Jones hit it out of bounds, and I won by a stroke."

He won with a 68, which tied the lowest final-round score ever made in the Open. Later in 1922, Sarazen won the PGA Championship. Two majors for a 20-year-old? Sarazen was indeed on his way. The next year, he successfully defended the PGA crown with a victory in the finals over his hero, Hagen.

At that time, the infant American pro tournament circuit offered very small purses, and Sarazen, who like Hagen was not interested in holding down a club job, made most of his income playing exhibitions. He put on a good show with his compact but powerful swing, and he was otherwise an innovative man who always found ways to promote himself and improve his game. He got much press when he insured his hands for well over $100,000. Putting poorly, he campaigned for a bigger hole—eight inches in diameter instead of 4¼. It was tried. It only made the good putters better, but Sarazen got plenty of "ink" for his idea. He would have another, more legitimate idea that everyone would adopt.

Like everyone of his generation, Sarazen was a poor sand bunker player because of the thin-bladed niblick (9-iron) that was used. Looking for an edge, Sarazen devised an angled flange for the back of the niblick so the club wouldn't dig into the sand so sharply. It was the first "sand wedge," as we have come to know it. Sarazen used it for the first

Sarazen, wrote Peter Alliss, "got more out of a small frame than either his contemporaries or successors. In his peak years from the early 1920s to the mid–1930s, only Jones, certainly, and Hagen, less obviously, were his superiors."

time to capture the 1932 British Open. The club was revolutionary in its impact on the playing of golf.

Sarazen won 38 tournaments in his time, 22 of them from 1925–31, and is one of only four players in history to win all four major championships. He managed to keep his game intact through 1940, when he lost in a playoff to Lawson Little for the U.S. Open, but after 1941 he was never again a contender. However, he always had a knack for the spectacular. On the par-5 15th hole in the last round of the 1935 Masters, Sarazen holed his 4-wood second shot. The double eagle got him into a tie with Craig Wood, and Sarazen wound up the victor. The spectacular shot is often credited with getting the Masters on its way as a major championship.

In 1960, Sarazen was "rescued" from the obscurity of the record books when he was signed to host a television series, *Shell's Wonderful World of Golf,* which was extremely popular and ran for 10 years on network television. It stimulated even more interest in the game and made everyone once again conscious of Gene Sarazen. But just to make sure, in making a farewell appearance in the 1973 British Open at the age of 71, Sarazen made a hole-in-one on the famed "Postage Stamp" par-3 at Royal Troon. The next day, with the television cameras now following his every move, he holed a bunker shot for a birdie on the very same hole. Sarazen went out with a flair, just as he had come in.

Left and below: *Having taught himself to play golf, Sarazen gripped the club in an unorthodox manner. His left hand was stronger than normal, and he placed his left thumb against the heel of his right hand instead of down the shaft. For average golfers, this would have spelled disaster off the tee.*

Patty Sheehan

Of the LPGA's top players in the 1980s and '90s, Patty Sheehan has been the most consistent performer. Starting in her first full season on the LPGA Tour, 1981, Sheehan won at least one tournament in every year except one through 1996. And she finished in the top 10 on the money list for 12 straight years, 1982–93.

Sheehan, who was born in Vermont and later moved to Nevada, was one of the top junior skiers in the country at age 13. She began to focus on golf, however, and won the first of four consecutive Nevada Amateurs at age 18 in 1975. She also won the California Amateur in 1978 and '79 and the national collegiate championship in 1980 while golfing for San Jose State. She was runner-up in the U.S. Women's Amateur in 1979.

Sheehan owns six titles in the three most important championships in women's golf, capturing three LPGA Championships (1983, '84, '93), two U.S. Women's Opens (1992, '94), and one Nabisco Dinah Shore (1996). She joined Mickey Wright (1960, '61) as the only back-to-back winners of the LPGA Championship, and Sheehan set the 18-hole tournament record with a 63 in 1984. Her most satisfying victories were the two Women's Opens, which came after finishing second in that event in 1983, '88, and '90. She lost a six-stroke lead after two rounds in 1990, but two years later she birdied the last two holes of regulation and then won a playoff against Juli Inkster.

Sheehan is considered to have one of the most natural swings in women's golf, which has helped her to avoid slumps. Though she has never led the money list, she has ranked second in earnings five times (1983, '84, '88, '90, and '93), was the Player of the Year in 1983, and won the Vare Trophy for low scoring average in 1984. Multiple wins in 10 seasons helped her to 35 career victories through 1996.

Sheehan's highest victory total, five, came in 1990, the year after her northern California home was destroyed by an earthquake. She later built a new home in Reno, Nevada.

Opposite page: *Sheehan takes a plunge after winning the 1996 Nabisco Dinah Shore. Below: Sheehan began cutting back on her tournament appearances in 1994 so she could spend more time at her home in Reno, Nevada, tending to her beloved garden.*

Horton Smith

No player in the history of the pro tour has gotten off to a faster start in his career than Horton Smith. The lanky Missourian came on the scene in 1928 and won a startling eight events during the 1928–29 winter tour when he was just 20 years old. He couldn't continue at that pace—indeed, no one ever has—but Smith went on to have a very good career, finishing with 31 victories and winning two of the first three Masters.

Smith was one of the best putters of his time, and he had a smooth swing—though some wondered why he always seemed to be experimenting with it. Perhaps he was trying to recapture the magic of 1928–29. His first two wins came late in 1928, and he scored a tour-high eight wins in 1929 (six early in the year and two late). Four more victories followed in 1930 before Smith hit a bit of a drought, winning just once in each of the next three years.

In 1934, Smith captured the inaugural Masters, getting a birdie on the 71st hole and finishing one stroke ahead of Craig Wood. He won the tournament in similar fashion in 1936, taking the lead on the next-to-last hole and beating Harry Cooper by one. Smith never captured the U.S. Open, finishing third in 1930 and 1940 after taking at least a share of the lead into the 36-hole final day each time. He also was third in the 1930 British Open.

Smith won two or three events each year from 1934–37, but he managed only two more wins after turning 30, both of them in 1941. He played the PGA Tour very little after World War II. Smith had become involved in tournament administration early in his career, becoming a member of the tournament committee as early as 1933. He served as president of the PGA from 1952–54. Smith is perhaps the first player to have used a club specifically designed for hitting the ball out of the sand, but the concave-face model he used was later banned.

Right: *Smith is pictured with his best club, his putter, which he used to capture the very first Masters tournament (then called the Augusta National Invitational).* Opposite page: *In one of his rare tournament appearances after the start of World War II, Lieut. Smith (left) arrives at Pinehurst on furlough from the Army in 1944. Clayton Heafner, a fellow pro golfer, accompanies him.*

A fine athlete who gave up football to pursue golf, Snead was "loose-jointed" with a full backswing and a graceful follow-through. This, coupled with his passion for the game, allowed him to compete into his 70s.

Sam Snead

An image of the golf swing that Sam Snead liked to project was: "It should feel oily." He spoke from personal experience, for Snead had one of the smoothest swings the game has ever known.

So fluid and full was Snead's swing, people thought he was double-jointed. Snead always smiled at the remark, enjoyed the compliment, but noted, "No one has double joints. I'm just loose-jointed. That's the proper way to put it." In fact, he was born with his vertebrae out of line. "I'd have been two inches taller if not for that," he said. Snead could have gone to college on an athletic scholarship in baseball or football, but his high school coach advised Sam that if he spent the four years in golf rather than in college, he would be further ahead. "I wanted to be an athlete," said Sam, and that he was.

His natural talent was monumental, and despite the misaligned vertebrae he was an amazing physical specimen who maintained his highest level of play for an uncommonly long period of time. Snead won his first tournament as a professional in 1936. He won his last on the regular PGA Tour, the Greater Greensboro Open, in 1965, when he was just short of his 53rd birthday. That made him the oldest winner ever on the Tour, a record that might well be etched in stone.

Samuel Jackson Snead was born in Hot Springs, Virginia, in 1912. He began caddying and playing golf at age seven at the famed Homestead Hotel, where his father worked as a maintenance engineer. A marvelous story teller, Snead once recalled in *Gettin' to the*

Snead takes a closer look at his putting line during play at the 1939 Masters, where he lost to Ralph Guldahl by one stroke. Guldahl played the last nine holes in 3-under-par to snatch the victory from Snead.

Snead won the Greater Greensboro Open eight times, which is an all-time record for most victories in a PGA Tour event. His last Greensboro victory came in 1965 when he was 52 years and 10 months old, which made him the oldest-ever winner on Tour.

Dance Floor: An Oral History of American Golf his first days at golf:

"My uncle used to come up on Sunday and get me by the hair and say, 'Come on, let's go pitch horseshoes. . . .' He couldn't beat me. So one day I was out back fooling around chipping—see, I put some tomato cans in the ground to make some holes and I'd chip with a jigger, which was like a 5-iron—and my uncle said, 'Gimme that,' meaning the jigger. So now we stopped playing horseshoes and started chipping. I beat him at that, too. Then one Sunday he came up with a bag of clubs, half left-handed, half right-handed, and said, 'C'mon, damn you, we're going up to the Goat.' That was the name of the little nine-hole course at the hotel where we could play. You'd play six holes up the mountain, and three of them off it. After a hole I'd ask my uncle, 'What'd you have, Uncle Ed?' He'd say he had a 5 or 4 and I'd say, 'Yeah, but you whiffed it down there a couple of times,' and he said, 'Son, those were practice swings,' and I said, 'No, you grunted. When you grunt, you made an effort and it counts.'

"That was my first golf, up and down the Goat. Oh, they wouldn't allow us on the regular courses—Cascades, Upper Cascades—but we'd slip on through a wooded area at the far end where a green was and chip and putt. If we saw somebody, we'd head for the brush."

It wasn't too long before Snead would be welcome at every great and famous golf course in the world. He started as a professional making clubs in the Homestead pro shop, also gave a few lessons, and then at age 20 was made the pro at the Cascades course. It was there that he began developing, or perfecting, his remarkably graceful swing and honing his championship game. "There hadn't been a pro there since the Crash of '29," Snead recalled. "So I had a chance to practice, and I beat sod. Oh, I beat sod. They said, 'Hey, you're beatin' all the grass off.' I broke the course record twice the first two weeks on the job."

Snead played on the PGA Tour for the first time in the 1935 Miami Open, making the trip in a Model A Ford. It took 2½ days to get there. "Going down through Georgia," Snead remembered, "there were one-way wooden bridges that might be 300 yards long and you had to look ahead to see if there was anyone at the other end coming on. If he was on first, then you'd have to wait your turn to get over." Two years later, Snead put together enough money to travel to California for the West Coast portion of the winter tour, and it was then that Snead's playing career, and public persona, emerged.

Snead won $600 in the Los Angeles Open. The next week, he won the Oakland Open, from which an anecdote was born that became the yardstick by which Snead's personality was measured for all time. His picture appeared in *The New York Times,* and upon seeing it Snead asked Tour manager Fred Corcoran how his picture got in a New York newspaper when he'd never been in that city. Corcoran, a master promoter of the Tour who knew a good line when he heard one—and who became Snead's business manager—never tired of relating that story. It brought attention to the circuit and established Snead as a kind of naive mountain boy. It worked, largely because Snead became one of the greatest players in the history of the game.

Snead won four more times in 1937, and the next year he won eight events on the circuit, a record total that would not be topped until

Above and left: *Thanks to his sweet stroke and even temperament, Snead lasted some four decades in the spotlight and drew large galleries, even on the practice range. "Watching Sam Snead practice hitting golf balls," said former pro John Schlee, "is like watching a fish practice swimming."*

A country bumpkin from the West Virginia foothills, Snead went to his first golf tournament with nine mismatched clubs costing $9. "The only reason I played golf," he said, "was so I could afford to hunt and fish."

1945. In '37, it appeared Snead would also win the U.S. Open. He shot a final-round 71 at Oakland Hills C.C., but a late rush by Ralph Guldahl (69) put Snead second by two strokes. It was the beginning of Snead's career-long disappointment in the national championship. He would win an official 81 tournaments on the PGA Tour, including three Masters and three PGA Championships—plus one British Open—yet he would never win the U.S. Open. He came close a number of times, including a playoff loss to Lew Worsham in 1947.

It was said that Snead lost his nerve for the most coveted of championships in 1939 by taking an 8 on the last hole when a 5 (par) would have brought him victory. Some would also suggest that because Snead never won the U.S. Open, he was not the complete champion that his arch rival, four-time U.S. Open winner Ben Hogan, was. And yet, in the three times Snead was in a playoff head-to-head against Hogan—including once for the Masters—he won every time.

Of the many comments Snead would make when asked about his U.S. Open record, the most incisive was: "When they say that I couldn't win the big one, I ask: What do you call all those others? What's big and what's small?" Indeed, Snead's seven triumphs in the modern majors is a number surpassed by only five other golfers. In 1946, he proved he could win in the granddaddy of tournaments, the British Open, on the grandest course, St. Andrews. He prevailed by a full four strokes.

Because of his incredible longevity as a first-class golfer, Snead was on the ground floor of, and a significant factor in, the development and growth of the Senior PGA Tour. In the first Legends of Golf event, the tournament that gave rise to the Senior circuit, Snead—on national television—put on a display of birdie golf on the final nine to bring him and his partner, Gardner Dickinson, an extremely popular and wonder-filled victory. At the age of 66, and by now finally retired from PGA Tour golf, Snead's swing was just as oily as ever as he outdrove and outplayed two golfers 17 years his junior—Peter Thomson and Kel Nagle—to win by a stroke.

Indeed, as a senior golfer, Snead won six PGA Seniors Championships, five World Seniors, and—in 1982 with Don January— yet another Legends of Golf tournament. He never grunted. Not once.

Putting troubled Snead. "A bad putter is like a bad apple in a barrel," he said. "First, it turns your chipping game sour. Then it begins to eat into your irons. And finally, it just eats the head off your driver."

Curtis Strange

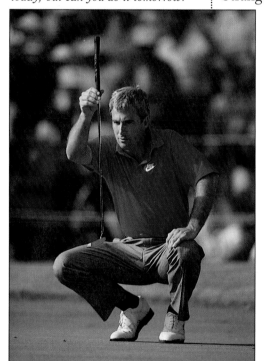

*O*nly six players have ever won back-to-back U.S. Open championships, and the only one to do so in the last 40 years is Curtis Strange. When he accomplished the feat in 1988–89, it was the signal achievement of a five-year span during which Strange won 12 tournaments and led the money list three times.

Strange's father, Tom, was a Virginia club professional who had played in the U.S. Open. He died when Curtis was 14. Strange built an outstanding amateur record, with his most impressive victory coming as a freshman at Wake Forest in the 1974 NCAA Championships. He eagled the final hole there to earn both the individual and team titles. Strange also won the 1973 Southeastern Amateur, the 1974 Western Amateur, the 1975 Eastern Amateur, and the 1975 and '76 North and South Amateurs. A long hitter in his amateur days, Strange throttled back when he turned pro in order to gain more control.

Strange left college in his junior year to turn pro in 1976, but he didn't score his first Tour win until the last event of 1979. He blossomed in 1985 when he won three times and led the money list. Strange's finest seasons came in 1987 and '88 when he led the Tour in earnings each year, totaling more than $2 million.

Going into the 1988 U.S. Open, Strange had done nearly everything except win a major championship. He finally claimed his first major at The Country Club, getting up-and-down from a bunker on the 72nd hole and then defeating Nick Faldo in a playoff. Strange defended the U.S. Open title the next year, passing a faltering Tom Kite on the final day at Oak Hill with a round that included 16 pars, one birdie, and one bogey.

Strange challenged for a third straight Open title in 1990 before dropping back in the final round. He later admitted he lost his motivation for the next couple of years, and he also had physical problems. His drive and his health later returned, but his game didn't make it all the way back. He remained winless in the 1990s.

Louise Suggs

*I*n the early days of the LPGA Tour, Louise Suggs said that watching herself, Patty Berg, and Babe Zaharias compete for tournament titles was like "watching three cats fight over a plate of fish." Suggs, a founding member of the LPGA, won her share, compiling 50 victories from 1949–62 to rank fifth on the all-time list.

Suggs was capable of some of the lowest scoring of her era. She shot a 291 total to win the 1949 U.S. Women's Open title by 14 strokes, still an LPGA record for victory margin. She won a second U.S. Open, in 1952, by seven strokes with a 284 total, albeit on a 5,460-yard, par-69 course.

Suggs, born in Atlanta in 1923, learned the game from her father at age 10 and won the Georgia Amateur when she was 16. She was an outstanding amateur, winning the North and South Amateur three times, sweeping the Western Amateur and Western Open in both 1946 and '47, and taking the Titleholders in 1946. Then came victories in the biggest amateur events on either side of the Atlantic, the U.S. Amateur in 1947 and the British championship in 1948. Suggs turned pro in the summer of 1948 rather than defend her U.S. Amateur title. But the Women's Professional Golf Association was foundering, and the next year Suggs became a charter member of the LPGA.

In addition to her two U.S. Women's Opens, Suggs won three Titleholders (1954, '55, and '59), two Western Opens (1949, '53), and one LPGA Championship (1957) for a total of eight major championships as a pro. She also was runner-up in five Women's Opens and four LPGA Championships. Her best stretch came in 1952, '53, and '54 when she won six, eight, and five tournaments. Suggs led the money list in 1953 and '60 and earned the Vare Trophy for low scoring average in 1957.

Suggs cut back her schedule after 1961, but as late as 1963, at age 39, she was second in both the U.S. Women's Open and LPGA Championship. She eventually served as LPGA president three times.

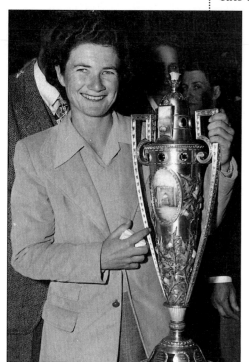

Above and opposite page: Suggs burst onto the national scene in 1946 when she won the Western Open. Nicknamed "Miss Sluggs" by Bob Hope, Suggs was a founder and charter member of the LPGA and among the first group of women elected to its Hall of Fame in 1951.

John H. Taylor

The British Army and Navy rejected John H. Taylor for poor eyesight, but their loss proved to be golf's gain. Taylor won five British Opens from 1894–1913, joining Harry Vardon and James Braid as part of the Great Triumvirate. His swing wasn't as graceful as Vardon's or as powerful as Braid's, but Taylor was considered the best putter of the three and was an excellent foul-weather player. He holds the British Open record for top-10 finishes with 23, including 17 in a row.

Taylor was born in England in 1871. He quit school at age 11 and worked at various jobs before becoming a greenkeeper. He entered his first British Open in 1893 and led after one round, then fell back. He won the next year at Sandwich in the first Open held in England, becoming the first of the Triumvirate to claim the title, and he successfully defended in 1895 at St. Andrews. Taylor nearly made it three in a row, but he dropped a playoff to Vardon in 1896.

Taylor won his third Open in 1900 in an eight-stroke romp at St. Andrews. That year, he made an exhibition tour of the United States with Vardon; in his only U.S. Open appearance, Taylor finished second to his countryman. Taylor became familiar with the runner-up spot in the British Open, finishing second four times in a row starting in 1904. He shot a record 68 in the final round in 1904 but fell one stroke short of Jack White. Conversely, he lost the 54-hole lead in 1906 and 1907.

Taylor regained his winning touch in 1909, taking the Open by four strokes. His final title came in 1913 when he won by eight in a driving storm. If he had played better in the final round in 1914, it would have been Taylor, not Vardon, with six Open championships. But Taylor faltered with a closing 83 as Vardon passed him. Taylor was the only one of the Triumvirate to contend in an Open after World War I, and he finished sixth as late as 1925 at age 54.

Below: *A fixture in British golf, Taylor also was highly regarded in the United States. Here, Taylor (left) arrives in the U.S. in 1922 with countryman Sandy Herd.* Opposite page: *As captain of Britain's 1933 Ryder Cup team, Taylor greets American captain Walter Hagen.*

Peter Thomson

Australia's Peter Thomson won only once in the United States, where he competed irregularly, but during the 1950s he reigned supreme in the British Open. Thomson finished with five British Open titles, a total surpassed by only Harry Vardon. His remarkable run included finishing first or second in seven consecutive years.

Thomson, born in 1929 in Melbourne, learned the game on his own as a teenager. His first tournament title came in the 1950 New Zealand Open. The next year, at age 21, he played in his first British Open and finished sixth. Then began his seven-year stretch of four wins and three seconds. Thomson was second in 1952 and '53, and he won three in a row beginning in 1954. He was the first to take three straight Opens since Robert Ferguson in the 19th century. After a runner-up finish in 1957, Thomson rebounded to take the 1958 title in a playoff over Dave Thomas.

Thomson won his fifth British Open in 1965, a satisfying victory because the top Americans were then making the trip to the British Open. That hadn't been the case in the 1950s, though international players Bobby Locke of South Africa and Roberto De Vicenzo of Argentina provided competition.

During the late 1950s, Thomson tried the U.S. circuit on occasion. His only victory came in the 1956 Texas International Open. He finished fourth in the 1956 U.S. Open after holding the 36-hole lead and was fifth in the 1957 Masters. Thomson never felt completely comfortable in the U.S. and its lush fairways; his low, running shots were better suited to links golf. Thomson won 26 events in Europe. He also captured nine New Zealand Opens and three Australian Opens.

With the birth of the Senior Tour in the 1980s, Thomson got a second chance in the U.S. He won 11 Senior tournaments, including the 1984 PGA Seniors Championship. His nine wins in 1985 set a Senior Tour record. Thomson, always a man with diverse interests (he once ran for the Victorian state senate), quit competing in the late 1980s while remaining active in course design and golf journalism.

Opposite page and above: *Thomson believed that golf was a game of mind over matter. "Certainly the difference between winning and losing, between the winner and the runner-up, is always a mental one," he said.*

Jerome Travers

Travers's trophy collection included hardware from one U.S. Open and four U.S. Amateurs —all four won by routs in the final match.

*O*ne of the game's most enigmatic champions, Jerome Travers is one of only two players to win at least four U.S. Amateur titles (Bobby Jones won five). Those victories came in 1907, '08, '12, and '13. Thought to excel only at match play, Travers pulled off a surprising victory in the 1915 U.S. Open, then retired from competition at the end of that year at age 28.

Travers was born on Long Island and came under the tutelage of Alex Smith at Nassau Country Club. He developed a rivalry with three-time U.S. Amateur champion Walter J. Travis, another Long Island resident. Travers, then 17, defeated the 42-year-old Travis in the 1904 Nassau Invitational. Travis knocked off Travers in the quarterfinal of the 1906 U.S. Amateur, but thereafter Travers had the edge on his older foe, beating him five times in the U.S. Amateur.

Travers's first two U.S. Amateur victories were romps in the finals, 6 & 5 over Archibald Graham in 1907 and 8 & 7 over Max Behr in 1908. Travers didn't enter the next two U.S. Amateurs. It is not known why, although it is possible that he chose to play only when he felt absolutely ready.

Travers returned in 1911, losing to eventual winner Harold Hilton, then won by large margins again in the next two years—7 & 6 over Chick Evans in 1912 and 5 & 4 over John Anderson in 1913. Travers lost in the final to Francis Ouimet in 1914.

Though he was one of the game's toughest competitors and owned an excellent short game, Travers was a wild driver and sometimes resorted to hitting irons off the tee. Before 1915, he had entered only three U.S. Opens, finishing no better than 25th. But that year at Baltusrol, he played the last six holes in 1-under to score a one-stroke victory over Tom McNamara. It was the last Open he played in. He didn't play in another U.S. Amateur either, saying it wasn't possible to both earn a living and play championship golf.

Travers was the closest thing to a dominant player in the decade preceding World War I, thanks in part to his calm demeanor. "I could always tell just from looking at a golfer whether he was winning or losing," said his instructor, Alex Smith, "but I never knew how Travers stood."

Walter Travis

*H*e didn't even play golf until he was 35 years old, but Walter Travis became one of the top figures in American golf at the start of the 20th century and was the first player from America to win the British Amateur.

Travis was actually born in Australia in 1862, but his family moved to the States when he was a boy. He didn't take up golf until 1897, but he caught on quickly— he reached the semifinals of the U.S. Amateur one year later. Travis also made the semifinals in 1899, then won the U.S. Amateur in 1900, '01, and '03. During that stretch, he won the qualifying medal in 1900, '01, and '02 (there was no qualifying in 1903).

Looking for another world to conquer, Travis decided to enter the 1904 British Amateur at Royal St. George's. He beat such top players as Harold Hilton and Horace Hutchinson on the way to the final, where he squared off against long-hitting Edward Blackwell. Travis was a short hitter, but he was deadly accurate and an outstanding putter. Those attributes carried him to a 4 & 3 victory. The win was not a popular one among his British hosts, who were put off by Travis's gruff manner. Travis, for his part, felt he had been given an unfriendly welcome. A few months later, the center-shafted Schenectady putter used by Travis in his victory was banned in Britain, though not in America.

By then, Travis was in his 40s, and he didn't win any more U.S. Amateurs (or enter any more British Amateurs). But he remained competitive for another decade, taking the qualifying medal in the 1906, '07, and '08 U.S. Amateurs and reaching the semifinals in 1906, '08, and '14. He won the 1915 Metropolitan Amateur at the age of 53.

Travis also made contributions to the game in other areas. He founded *The American Golfer* magazine in 1908 and served as its editor for many years. He became involved in designing courses, including Garden City Golf Club on Long Island and Westchester Country Club just north of New York City.

Opposite page and above: *The cigar-chomping Travis was especially effective in match play, where his impeccable short game and putting gave him the edge. Nicknamed the "Old Man" after taking up golf in his 30s, he was dubbed the "Grand Old Man" in his later years.*

Lee Trevino

Trevino rose from poverty to the pinnacle of professional golf. He never knew his father and was raised by his mother and grandfather, neither of whom could read or write.

*L*ee Trevino's first experience in golf was as a pre-teen hunting golf balls hit out of bounds into a field near where he lived—a simple four-room wooden house with no electricity or plumbing. There was nowhere for him to go but up. He did on the strength of an overwhelming desire to do just that. He made himself a man of means playing a game at which he worked very hard.

Born in 1939 in Dallas, Lee Buck Trevino was raised by his mother and a grandfather. He left school after the eighth grade to earn money for the family by working at a par-3 course. After serving four years as an enlistee in the Marine Corps, Trevino returned to work at the par-3 as well as at a driving range. But he made more money wagering on himself at golf—and not all of it the "traditional" kind. His most famous hustle was hitting his shots with the fat end of a taped-up Dr Pepper bottle and putting with the thin end, a la billiards.

As his game with real clubs improved, the bets got bigger and so did the competition. Once in the early 1960s, Raymond Floyd—already a nationally known golfer who also liked to play high-stakes golf off the PGA Tour—got hooked up in Texas against a fellow named Trevino. Floyd left lighter in his wallet, and he was glad to be free of the then-unknown Mexican-American with the tattoos who putted with the fine touch of a safecracker and had even more nerve. Of course, Floyd would not be free of Trevino, nor would any other Tour golfer.

In his formative years, Trevino had a "classic" swing, but it just didn't work. He hooked the ball badly under pressure. Then one day he watched from afar Ben Hogan practicing, and he liked the

Even if he missed a green by a wide margin, the scrambling Trevino felt he could get the ball into the hole in two more strokes. Here he searches for a path to the green from the trees during a winning effort at the 1984 PGA Championship at Shoal Creek.

Right and far right: *"No one who ever had lessons would have a swing like mine,"* said Trevino, who early in his career was rejected as a golf outsider. *"I played the Tour in 1967 and told jokes and nobody laughed,"* he said. *"Then I won the Open the next year, told the same jokes, and everybody laughed like hell."*

controlled left-to-right fade Hogan hit, one after another. Trevino decided that flight pattern was for him, and for five years, on his own, he worked on a way to accomplish it. In the end, it didn't look at all like Hogan's swing, if only because of Trevino's short, chunky physique, but he got the same result. And then some. No one questions the assessment that Trevino became the best ball-striker since Hogan. In the 1990s, he was once asked when he last hit a ball out of bounds. In all sincerity, he couldn't remember. Nor could anyone else.

Trevino turned professional in 1960, but he somehow never joined the PGA of America and thus did not qualify to play on the Tour, then run by that organization. He had to play in open events, and in 1965 he won the highly competitive Texas State Open. In his first U.S. Open, in 1966, he made the cut and finished 54th. He continued to practice, give some lessons at an El Paso club where he was an assistant pro, and hustle on the golf course to take care of a growing family by his first wife. It was she who suggested Trevino enter the 1967 U.S. Open, being played in New Jersey.

Trevino scraped together some money, lived inexpensively far from the course (Baltusrol G.C.), and made his name known for the first time outside of Texas by finishing a very solid fifth in the championship. With the $6,000 he took in, and a showing that enabled him to get into subsequent Tour events that year, Trevino won another $20,000.

He was set, financially and game-wise, to begin his invasion of major-league professional golf. He was indeed an overnight sensation.

At the 1968 U.S. Open, Trevino stayed close to the lead through three rounds, then canned two birdie putts at the 65th and 66th holes with a combined length of 55 feet to ice victory. He became the first to ever win a U.S. Open with all four rounds in the 60s. The brilliant golf, combined with a quick and funny wit delivered with the panache of a stand-up comic, turned Trevino into a gallery favorite.

From 1968–84 on the PGA Tour, Trevino won 27 times, including another U.S. Open (in a playoff with Jack Nicklaus) and two PGA Championships, the last coming at the age of 44. Not even lightning could stop him. Trevino (along with golfers Jerry Heard and Bobby Nichols) was struck by lightning during play in the 1975 Western Open. Still, at 36, he recovered enough to win nine more PGA Tour events, including his second PGA Championship (sixth major) and 26 Senior Tour events from 1990–95. Near the end of 1995, however, Trevino had major back surgery in which a permanent plate was inserted through his neck to fuse disks.

The back problem may have derived in part from the lightning bolt, but more likely it resulted from having hit hundreds of practice balls every day, day in and day out, for years. All the hard work had finally caught up with him, but by then the poor kid from the other side of the tracks had become a multimillionaire—and one of the most accomplished and popular golfers the game has ever seen.

Trevino's income skyrocketed after he joined the Senior Tour. "One of the nice things about the Senior Tour," he joked, "is that we can take a cart and a cooler. If your game is not going well, you can always have a picnic."

Harry Vardon

In 1900, Harry Vardon, a 30-year-old Englishman born on the Isle of Jersey, played an extensive exhibition tour of the United States. It was meant to promote interest in what was still a very new game to the United States, while at the same time publicize a new golf ball, the Vardon Flyer, made by the A. G. Spalding Co. Vardon was chosen because he was the best golfer in the world. The year before, Vardon had won his third British Open (he would win six Opens, a record to this day).

The choice of Vardon served the purpose of inspiring people to take up the game because of his smooth and elegant swing. Vardon, who was sometimes referred to as "The Greyhound," is considered the "father of the modern golf swing." He was the first to make a science of the swing, working out mechanics that everyone could understand and try to emulate. He did not in fact invent the golf grip named after him—in which the little finger of the lower hand on the club overlaps the index finger of the opposite hand—but he is certainly responsible for its dissemination. The Vardon Grip, which Vardon said best unified the hands for a more consistent swing, is to this day used by the majority of the world's golfers. Vardon was also known for his accuracy, which he allied with considerable power, but it was the latter that his first American audiences admired most.

Above: Vardon (right) poses with countryman Ted Ray at the 1913 U.S. Open. Vardon and Ray were upset by long shot Francis Ouimet, an amateur, in a three-way playoff. Opposite page: "The father of the modern golf swing" watches the flight of his ball. Harry's Vardon Grip is still used by most golfers.

Vardon recalled in a book about his first trip to America: "At that period, the Americans were not sufficiently advanced [in golf] to appreciate the finer points of the game. They did, however, appear to thoroughly enjoy the type of ball I drove. I hit it high for carry, which resembled a home run."

For his 1900 tour of the United States, Vardon traveled over 20,000 miles, going as far west as Chicago and throughout the Southeastern states. Except for a break to return home to defend his British Open title (he finished second), his 1900 tour extended through most of the year. At each stop, he played the "best ball" of the two best players in the town, or a top professional in a singles contest. He lost only 13 out of 65 best-ball matches and dropped only one singles match. In grand fashion, Vardon won the 1900 U.S. Open (even though he whiffed at a one-inch putt on the final hole). Vardon prevailed by two strokes and outdistanced the nearest American professional, David Ball, by 10 shots.

The 1900 tour has rightfully been credited with creating the first significant interest in golf in the United States. Vardon would return again to the United States, in 1913, for another exhibition tour. With this trip, he was again a factor in arousing interest in golf by Americans, but this time because he lost a competition. That year, Vardon (and his compatriot, Ted Ray) were defeated in a playoff for the U.S. Open by a young, unknown American amateur named Francis Ouimet. Had Ouimet beaten someone of less repute than Vardon (and Ray), his victory would hardly have gotten the acclaim it did—acclaim that spurred one of the biggest booms in American golf annals.

Vardon, along with his brothers, got into golf as a caddie. He played his first golf at the age of eight when he, his brothers, and other young boys built a course of their own. (Most of the holes were in the 50-yard-long

"There were stylists no doubt before Harry Vardon," said Henry Cotton, "but he—because his swing seemed to give as good or better results than any contemporary with less apparent effort—was known as 'the stylist.'"

range.) He made his own clubs—the heads of oak, the faces covered with strips of tin, the shafts of blackthorn branches. The "balls" were marbles.

Vardon followed his father into gardening work. But his first job was for a retired Army officer who was a golf fanatic, and he gave Vardon his first set of real golf clubs. Not long after, in his early 20s, Vardon followed his brother into professional golf. In 1896, the 26-year-old Vardon won his first British Open title, defeating defending champion J. H. Taylor by four strokes in a 36-hole playoff. Vardon remained at the top of the game for the next 25 years. Much of his competitive record has been lost, but it is known that at one point he had won 14 straight tournaments in Great Britain.

Putting wasn't Vardon's strong suit. "I think I know as well as anybody how not to do it," he once said. However, Vardon's accuracy is the stuff of legend. It was said that if he played the same course in the afternoon that he played that morning, the second time around he hit out of his morning divots. Perhaps not, but

Vardon traveled far and wide as a golf ambassador, playing tournaments, promoting the game, and dispensing sage advice. "When practicing," he liked to say, "use the club that gives you the most trouble, not the one that gives you the most satisfaction."

such stories usually have some basis in fact. Whatever the case, Vardon was an exceptionally straight shooter—in manner as well as with his golf clubs. He was a taciturn man, soft-spoken but trenchant when the moment arose. A young Bobby Jones was paired with Vardon in a qualifying round for the 1920 U.S. Open. And after Jones topped a simple pitch shot, he asked Vardon, "Did you ever see a worse shot in your life?" To which Vardon answered, simply and honestly, "No."

Ken Venturi

His shining moment came in a courageous victory while battling heat exhaustion at the 1964 U.S. Open, but it should also be noted that Ken Venturi was one of the Tour's best players during the late 1950s. He won 14 tournaments in a PGA Tour career that ended prematurely due to a circulatory problem in his hands.

Venturi, born in San Francisco in 1931, was runner-up in the first U.S. Junior championship in 1948. Venturi nearly won the 1956 Masters as an amateur, taking a four-stroke lead into the final round before collapsing with an 80 in windy conditions to finish second, one stroke behind Jack Burke Jr.

Venturi, who turned pro later in 1956, would come close in two more Masters. He finished fourth, two strokes off the lead, in 1958, and he was second by one stroke in 1960 thanks to Arnold Palmer's finish of birdies on the last two holes. Nonetheless, Venturi finished in the top 10 on the money list in his first four years on Tour, 1957–60, winning 10 events in that span.

Venturi had gained a reputation as one of the best iron players in the game. However, after 1960, he decided to make some changes to gain more length off the tee. His game lost consistency and he went into a deep slump. Venturi began to return to form in 1964, but he was still a long shot at the U.S. Open. Venturi was two strokes behind after a third-round 66 at Congressional. By the end of the round, the 100-degree heat was beginning

Venturi is pictured in his trademark white linen cap. At one time, he was touted as the next Ben Hogan, but injuries and faulty swing mechanics scuttled his bid for greatness and limited him to 14 Tour victories.

to get to him, and there was some question whether Venturi would be able to complete the 36-hole final day. With a doctor following him, Venturi managed to get around with a closing 70 to win by four.

He won three more events in 1964, but the next year Venturi was struck by the circulatory problem. He had surgery and missed most of the campaign. He came back with one win in 1966, but the ailment still dogged him. Venturi soon retired from competition and became a fixture in the CBS broadcast booth.

Venturi's victory at the 1964 U.S. Open halted what Sports Illustrated *called "a three-year slide to oblivion." On the verge of quitting, Venturi pocketed just $3,848 in 1963 and failed to earn an invitation to the 1964 Masters. His Open victory was keyed by a sparkling 30 on the front nine of the third round, the greatest nine holes of his career.*

Tom Watson

Only one golfer ever came close to challenging Jack Nicklaus as the most dominant player in golf. That was Tom Watson, who from 1974–83 won eight major championships and 28 tournaments overall on the PGA Tour. In the same time frame, Nicklaus won six majors (and 18 PGA Tour events). To be sure, Nicklaus had been on the tournament circuit for 12 years when Watson won for the first time on the PGA Tour—the 1974 Western Open—and had cut back on his schedule of appearances to some extent, but Nicklaus's capacity for great golf, and the longevity of it, was so colossal that the comparison between the two is valid.

Thomas Sturges Watson was born in Kansas City, Missouri, in 1949. Although a most promising golfer from the start, Watson did not have an especially remarkable amateur career. He won his share of smaller amateur events, but none of the prestigious ones. And in playing for the Stanford University team, he did not shine as his future record would suggest he should have.

It took him three years on the PGA Tour, which he joined in 1971, to win for the first time. When he did have a chance to win a major title, he showed a tendency to weaken down the stretch. He led the 1974 U.S. Open by a shot after three rounds, but he finished with a 79 to end up tied for fifth. The next year, in the Open, he opened with rounds of 67–68 to take a three-stroke lead, but he shot 78–77 to finish in a tie for ninth. After this, he was considered something of a choker. He proceeded to put the slur to rest, with a fury.

In 1975, Watson broke through to win the British Open, in a playoff with Jack Newton. Winning his first major in Great Britain was fitting, for Watson always had a particular affinity for playing there. The often wet weather smacked so much of the golf he played growing up in Missouri. Also, he had always expressed a fondness for the grand traditions

Opposite page: *Watson rejoices with his caddie after a dramatic victory in the 1975 British Open at Carnoustie.* Above: *"Charisma," Watson said, "is winning major championships."*

In his prime, Watson was a master of approach shots and the short game. "If he's lying 6 in the middle of the fairway," quipped Lee Trevino, "there's some kind of way he might make 5."

of the old Scots' game. Indeed, he would win the British Open five times (1975, '77, '80, '82, and '83). Only one other player, Peter Thomson, has won that honored title that many times in the modern era.

All golfers' careers in the Nicklaus Era were naturally measured against Jack's, and Watson had two significant high points. In 1982 at Pebble Beach, it appeared Nicklaus would win his fifth U.S. Open. But Watson chipped in from a heavy lie in the fringe off the 17th green for a birdie-2 and a one-shot lead, which he maintained. The chip-in was an unforgettable moment. But the two of them had already gone one better.

In the 1977 British Open at Turnberry, Scotland, Watson's victory over Nicklaus was the most dynamic one-on-one confrontation in golf history. They both shot 68–70 in rounds one and two, then the fireworks began. Watson and Nicklaus, playing together, matched 65s in round three. Again together for the final 18, they had left the field so far behind that when they came to the 72nd hole, either one of them could 10-putt and finish runner-up.

Leading by a stroke going to the last hole, Watson drove perfectly in the fairway. Nicklaus drove into deep gorse. Watson played an 8-iron approach to within 30 inches of the hole. Miraculously, Nicklaus freed his ball from the thicket with an 8-iron, the ball finishing 32 feet from the cup. He then ran the putt in for a round of 66. He had beaten the British Open 72-hole scoring record by seven shots—and still lost. Watson holed for a 65.

Watson also won two Masters, both in duels with Nicklaus. In the final round in 1977, Nicklaus caught up with Watson at the 13th hole. But when Watson holed a 20-foot birdie putt at 17, Nicklaus wilted (at 18), and Watson won by two. He won it again in 1981 by two over Nicklaus and Johnny Miller.

Watson would continue his powerful, well-thought-out golf through 1984, when he won three times on the PGA Tour, but then his game went into a steep decline. It was almost as if all the bold putting that was his trademark had caught up with his nerves. His putting approach continued to be aggressive, but all of a sudden he could no longer make the three- and four-footers coming back. Perhaps he needed Nicklaus to inspire him, but by the mid-1980s Jack was finally beginning to wind down his competitive career.

Interestingly, while Watson's ball-striking got better and better—his tendency toward wildness off the tee had been well tamed—his putting from short distances under ultimate pressure got worse and worse. He became a rather sympathetic figure as he missed one after another in the clutch, and a new generation of younger stars was beginning to emerge. He continued to fight the good fight, though, and in 1996 won for the first time in nine years. Ironically, the victory came at the Memorial Tournament, an event begun by, and played on a course designed by, Jack Nicklaus.

Watson celebrates winning the 1996 Memorial, breaking a nine-year winless streak. Watson contended in numerous tournaments during that period, but shaky putting down the stretch often did him in.

Kathy Whitworth

*I*n a world with the collective attention span that's the length of a television commercial, Kathy Whitworth's career may not seem noteworthy. But for those who understand and appreciate the strength involved in upholding a well-honed athletic talent—and the determination to maintain a high standard for achievement for over four decades—then Whitworth will always be reassuring.

Kathrynne Ann Whitworth was born in Monahans, Texas, in 1939 and raised in Jal, New Mexico, where her father and mother ran a hardware store. A natural athlete, and inclined to play sports despite the social stigma this meant for someone of her gender in her generation, she took up golf at the age of 15 and showed enough promise from the start that a teacher of the highest repute took her on as a student—the great Harvey Penick. At 19, Whitworth won her second consecutive New Mexico State Amateur championship and left a college in Odessa, Texas, where she had a golf scholarship, to turn pro.

Whitworth's father and two businessmen friends promised her a three-year sponsorship on the LPGA Tour, which was just beginning to get on its feet. Moreover, Wilson Sporting Goods signed her to a contract that included paying her expenses plus a stipend for doing golf clinics, and she was on her way. Whitworth seemed set to light up the women's golf world right from the start, but her fuse happened to be a slow one. In her first season on the circuit, 1959, she entered 26 events and won a grand total of $1,217 on the basis of a scoring average of 80.30.

Opposite page and below: *Tutored by teaching pros Harvey Penick and Hardy Loudermilk, Whitworth crafted a steady, consistent swing and tremendous accuracy. She had excellent staying power, too, as evidenced by her 88 victories from 1962–85. Many consider her the greatest woman golfer of modern times.*

Perhaps the biggest putt of Whitworth's career occurred at the 1967 LPGA Championship at Pleasant Valley Country Club in Massachusetts. She holed a 50-footer for birdie on the 72nd hole to win by one stroke over Shirley Englehorn.

Nevertheless, she hung in there to become the biggest winner in American golf history.

It is difficult to imagine that the tall, slender, tautly muscled woman fans saw for so many years weighed over 200 pounds when she was in high school. "I'd probably be the fat lady in the circus if it hadn't been for golf," Whitworth once said. "It kept me out of the refrigerator." As she gradually pared down to her playing weight, 145, which she maintained throughout her career, her game improved accordingly. In 1962, Whitworth won her first LPGA tournament, the Kelly Girl Open, and won one more that season. In 28 appearances in '62 (she was a workhorse, playing an average of 25 tournaments a year from 1959–91), she hit double figures for the first time in money won on the year—$17,044.

Although not a very long hitter of the ball, Whitworth was long enough for her time. More important, she put together a very functional and repeatable golf swing. It wasn't the kind that lasts for the ages, and it wasn't the flowing poetry in motion of Mickey Wright, but neither was it Nancy Lopez's exotic manifestation. It was right down the middle, which is where Whitworth played most of her golf. The Whitworth swing held up very well.

In 1963, Whitworth won eight tournaments. She had a quiet '64, with only one victory, but in 1965 she won eight more times, including her first major, the Titleholders Championship, which she won again the next year. In 1967, she won eight events including two more majors—the LPGA Championship and the Western Open. She was on a long and good roll, but after her 1973 season, when she won seven times, the physical and emotional strain of playing at such a high level for a decade did take its toll. She even had a notion to pack it in. But it was only a notion, it was not Whitworth, and she came back to win again and again. In all, she won 88 LPGA events, which is the all-time record among both men and women.

It is a curious coincidence that just as Sam Snead on the men's side won more tournaments than any other of his gender (81 officials plus a British Open) but never won the U.S. Open, so it was with Kathy Whitworth, who never could take the U.S. Women's Open. And just as in Snead's case, the missing major in her record doesn't at all diminish Whitworth's career.

What's more, it should be added that while accumulating her competitive record, Whitworth held at one time or another every LPGA administrative office at least once—from treasurer to three-time president—a time- and energy-consuming labor that Snead and the other greats never had to take on. Whitworth joined the LPGA circuit in the days when it was run by the players themselves, with everyone pitching in to lure sponsors, organize the events, and in some cases even cut the holes. And yet, while performing her various organizational duties, she was the leading money winner eight times and won the Vare Trophy (for low stroke average) seven times. Though her winning purses were as low as $800, Whitworth won so much that she became the first woman to reach $1 million in career prize money.

The presence of Mickey Wright delayed Whitworth's rise to the top of the LPGA money list. In 1962, for example, Whitworth was the runner-up to Wright in five tournaments, including three in a row.

Tiger Woods

Not since Jack Nicklaus came onto the scene three-and-a-half decades earlier had the golf world seen anything like Tiger Woods. Like Nicklaus, Woods compiled an outstanding amateur record, and instant success was expected when he hit the PGA Tour. Like Jack, Tiger delivered, winning a major championship in his first year as a pro. And, like the young Nicklaus, Woods hit the ball so much farther than other pros that he seemed to be playing a different game.

In fact, while it can't be known whether he will have the staying power to challenge Nicklaus's record total of 18 major professional championships, Woods made an even bigger impact on the game in his first year as a pro than the Golden Bear did. For one thing, Woods is part African American (also part Asian and a small part American Indian), which is significant because there were no black players on the Tour full-time when he arrived. Also, he plays an exciting, attacking style and has a charismatic smile. When Woods is in a tournament, attendance and television ratings go through the roof. Woods has the kind of mass appeal that brings new players to the game, much like Arnold Palmer had.

If any golfer were ever destined for greatness from an early age, it was Woods. Tiger, who grew up in the Los Angeles suburbs and learned to swing the club by mimicking his father, Earl, made his first trip to the driving range at 18 months. At age two, he won a 10-and-under tournament and appeared on the *Mike Douglas Show*. At eight, he broke 80 for the first time. At 12, he broke 70. At 14, he started winning national junior tournaments for players 17 and under.

Above: Woods made history in 1997 when he shattered Jack Nicklaus's Masters record by 12 strokes. Opposite page: Tiger bears down on a putt in the 1997 Westchester Classic.

Woods's greatest amateur accomplishments came in USGA events. Before him, no player had won the U.S. Junior Amateur more than once. Woods won it three times in a row at ages 15 (the youngest ever to win it), 16, and 17. He followed that by becoming the youngest-ever U.S. Amateur champion, at 18. When he won the U.S. Amateur again at 19 and 20, he became the first player ever to win that event three straight times.

Many of those wins came in dramatic fashion. In his third U.S. Junior victory, Woods was two down with two holes to play, birdied them both, and won on the first extra hole. He won his first U.S. Amateur by coming from six down after 13 holes of the 36-hole final to take a 2-up victory over Trip Kuehne. He captured his third by charging from five down after 18 to win on the 38th hole against Steve Scott.

By then, Woods had completed two years at Stanford, winning one NCAA Championship, and speculation centered on how soon he would turn pro. Woods took that step immediately following his third U.S. Amateur victory, encouraged by many top pros telling him he was ready for the Tour and sensing that college and amateur golf would no longer hold enough interest for him. Nike immediately gave him a $40 million endorsement contract. At the time, many wondered if Woods deserved it, since

Above and right: *Fans flock to witness Tiger in action. Even fellow pros are amazed. As was once said about the "Golden Bear" himself, "He's playing a game with which we are not familiar," said Jack Nicklaus about Woods. "He hits the ball nine million miles and without a swing that looks like he's trying to."*

he hadn't yet proved himself on the Tour. He quickly demonstrated that he was worth every penny—and more.

Playing in only eight tournaments in 1996 after turning pro at the end of August, he won twice (the Las Vegas Invitational and Walt Disney World/Oldsmobile Classic), finished

Woods has had a lot to smile about lately. Here he shares a moment of mirth with Kevin Costner at the AT&T Pebble Beach National Pro-Am. And the future looks wide open for this young phenom. "I think he can win almost anywhere," said Arnold Palmer. "I don't think there's anything that can stop him."

third twice, and collected $790,594. He was a phenomenon in every sense of the word. Even his fellow pros were in awe of his distance off the tee, accomplished with the efficiency of his swing rather than brute strength (he's 6'2", 155 pounds). And he brought the spectators flooding through the gates, particularly youngsters who wouldn't have otherwise been interested in golf.

Tigermania continued in 1997. He won the first tournament of the year, the Mercedes Championships, by nearly holing his tee shot to win a sudden-death playoff. At the Masters, he topped even the loftiest expectations by blowing away the field with a record 72-hole total of 270 to win by a record 12 strokes. By then, it was clear that the sky was the limit.

Mickey Wright

*I*t is usually the case that the greatest golfers do not swing by the "book," but succeed through guile and determination. On the other hand, most of those who do make a smooth and elegant classic swing, with everything falling into the right places, never possess the intangibles to reach the greatest heights. It follows then that if someone combines a perfect golf swing with an intense will to win, that someone is going to be very special. Such a person was Mary Kathryn "Mickey" Wright, who to this day is heralded as the all-time greatest woman golfer. Her record is proof of that. And thanks to film and video, golfers not born when Wright was in her prime are able to view and confirm for themselves her exquisite expression of the golfing art.

Wright was born in San Diego in 1935. At the age of nine, she played her first golf and "took to it like a duck," as Wright once recalled. Only two years later, after she broke 100 for the first time, her picture appeared in a San Diego newspaper with a caption: "The Next Babe?" "From that time on, I was determined to become a professional golfer," said Wright. Her first formal instruction was with Johnny Bellante, who also got Gene Littler started.

When Wright was 14, she broke 70 for the first time and also won the Southern California Girls' Junior championship. The pro at the venue for that event was Harry Pressler, a highly regarded teacher, and Wright began taking lessons from Pressler. It was he who was mainly responsible for shaping the Wright swing. But Wright, an inveterate student of the golf swing, would also work with Stan Kertes (who taught Babe Zaharias to play) and Texas pro Earl Stewart. So she found the best teachers, to which she added her own intelligence and natural physical gifts. A tallish woman, with a slender and neatly proportioned figure, she had a long

Opposite page and above: *Rated as the greatest long-ball hitter in women's golf, the sweet-swinging Wright fashioned an incredible five-year hot spell. In each season from 1960–64, she won the Vare Trophy for the lowest stroke average. She amassed 50 tournament victories during that span.*

Wright began practicing on a driving range at age nine and played her first round two years later. She scored 145. She broke 100 when she was 11, and 80 when she was 13.

swing arc and the powerful hand action at impact associated with men players. Both were sources of her considerable length off the tee. And, with her uncomplicated swing pattern, she was also very accurate—not to mention consistent.

As an amateur on the national level, Wright won the 1952 U.S. Girls' Junior and the 1954 World Amateur. She was also the low amateur in the 1954 U.S. Women's Open. She attended Stanford University for a year, at the insistence of her father, but was not happy. She just wanted to play golf, professionally. Her father could not ignore her accomplishments and relented. He gave Mickey $1,000 to get started, and the great odyssey began. Wright turned pro in 1955 and won her first LPGA tournament in 1956. She won thrice in 1957, but in that year's U.S. Open made, in retrospect, an incredibly poor showing with rounds of 79–82–81–80. The next year, she made up for it in a major way.

In 1958, Wright won three regular Tour events plus the LPGA Championship and the U.S. Open. In the latter, she became at 23 the youngest winner of the championship. She led after every round, finished five shots ahead of Louise Suggs, and set a new Open scoring record with a 2-under-par 290—one better than Babe Zaharias scored in 1954. The question asked in the photo caption in the San Diego newspaper 12 years before was answered. The next year, Wright defended her U.S. Open title and broke her own scoring record by three shots. She would win the Open four times and claim a total of 13 majors.

Wright's competitive record is filled with striking achievements: second in all-time LPGA victories with 82; winner of three majors in one season—the 1961 U.S. Women's Open, LPGA, and Titleholders; twice recorded four consecutive victories on the LPGA Tour (1962 and '63); and won 13 times in 1963, a stratospheric record in the Byron Nelson class that many feel will never be equaled.

Wright did all her marvelous playing from 1956–69, then stopped playing regularly owing to some real and, some would say, self-designed reasons: She had developed a growth on her left foot, and after an operation played all her golf in tennis shoes. She also suffered from sheer exhaustion; sponsors threatened to cancel tournaments if she didn't appear, and in acceding for the good of the circuit she played more than anyone should. She also claimed an adverse reaction to the sun, as well as an aversion to flying (which became necessary as the LPGA Tour grew, thanks in good part to her). Finally, Wright had an abiding modesty that never allowed her enjoy her celebrity. A quiet, introspective woman with a range of interests outside of golf (literature, music, fishing, the stock market), she became something of a recluse in Florida.

In 1979, however, Wright competed in the Coca-Cola Classic and got into a five-way playoff that was eventually won by 22-year-old Nancy Lopez. Wright, at 44, hadn't competed consistently for a decade, but she outhit Lopez off the tee and outplayed the three others in the overtime play before losing on the second extra hole to a birdie—if "losing" is the right word for it.

Like her idol, Babe Didrikson Zaharias, Wright was a powerful driver. During one tournament in 1960, aided by a strong wind, she overdrove the green on a 385-yard hole.

Babe Didrikson Zaharias

*I*t is the rare athlete who can master more than one sport, and even more so when the transition is to golf. Mildred "Babe" Didrikson Zaharias managed it, although in considering her immense athletic talent, it is not that surprising.

Didrikson was an All-America basketball player in high school, a proficient swimmer and diver, an expert rifle shot, a boxer, a speed-ball softball pitcher, a top-notch bowler, and a tennis player of championship caliber. Track and field, however, was where she made her initial impact on the sports world. In the 1932 national track and field championships, she placed first in eight of 10 events she entered. It was two weeks later that the young Texan became a truly international star. In the 1932 Olympic Games in Los Angeles, Didrikson placed first in two events and a controversial second in another. In going for the gold, she set a new world record in the javelin throw, broke the old world record for the 80-meter hurdles in winning her heat, then broke that record in the finals. She tied for first in the high jump but was then penalized for diving over the bar head first; she settled for the silver medal.

Cashing in on her new-found fame, Didrikson played the vaudeville circuit for a time, dancing and playing the harmonica. (At age seven, she had been a harmonica soloist on a Texas radio station, and she was a professional-level tap dancer.) More interested in sports, Babe left show business and played on a professional basketball team as well as some exhibition baseball. She pitched for the House of David team and threw an inning's worth for the Philadelphia Phillies in an exhibition game against the Brooklyn Dodgers.

Opposite page: *Even before the 1932 Olympics, Mildred Ella Didrikson was considered the world's greatest woman athlete.* Above: *Babe won two gold medals and set two world records at the 1932 Games.*

GOLF LEGENDS OF ALL TIME

Above: *Besides golf, Didrikson excelled in virtually every sport she tried. She once threw a baseball a reported 313 feet, and she even toured the country in billiards exhibitions.* Right: *Babe's husband, George Zaharias, was a professional wrestler nicknamed "The Greek from Cripple Creek."*

Then, in 1934, Didrikson turned to golf, which she had been playing on and off for a number of years and for which she, of course, exhibited a tremendous talent. In 1935, Didrikson (she would add Zaharias to her name in 1938 after marrying George Zaharias, a professional wrestler) went on a golf exhibition swing with Gene Sarazen. Although not yet a finished golfer, she could hit the ball distances equal to that of many men players. Her power was a great attraction and amplified her nickname, "Babe," which came after she hit five home runs in a baseball game. "When I want to really blast one," she once said, "I just loosen my girdle and let 'er fly." However, if she was going to compete in golf at a championship level, she would have to refine the rest of her game. Zaharias took lessons from Stan Kertes, a fine, albeit unheralded golf teacher in Chicago and Los Angeles. She practiced long and hard for a couple of years and began entering a few tournaments.

Born in Port Arthur, Texas, in 1911, the daughter of Norwegian immigrants, she was Babe Zaharias for most of her competitive golf career, which began in earnest during the World War II years (1942–45). Declared a professional (for her baseball and basketball earnings) after winning the Women's Texas Invitational in 1935, her amateur status was reinstated in 1943, at her request. In 1945, she won her third Western Open. In 1946 and '47, she won 14 amateur tournaments in a row, including the '46 U.S. Women's Amateur and the '47 British Women's Amateur. She was the first American ever to take the latter, and afterwards she again

became a professional, this time for good.

In the late 1940s, Zaharias, Patty Berg, and Betty Hicks re-formed the Women's Professional Golf Association into the Ladies PGA, and they began developing its tour. Zaharias was a major attraction by virtue of her excellent golf, but also as an outgoing, irrepressible personality. Her show-business instincts and actual background were never far from the surface. From 1948–55, Zaharias won 31 professional tournaments, including three U.S. Women's Opens.

Zaharias's professional golf career was actually rather short —only nine years—because her

Babe pauses to heat some of her irons in a furnace to "take the chill off my game," she said. Asked how she hits the ball so far, she said, "When I want to really blast one, I just loosen my girdle and let 'er fly."

fabled physical capacities began to deteriorate. In 1952, she had surgery for a strangulated hernia. Then, in April 1953, she was operated on for cancer. Her doctor said she would never play championship golf again. But, of course, he underestimated the Babe. Three months later she was back on Tour, and the following year she won five times, including her third U.S. Open, which she won by an astonishing 12 strokes over Hicks. In '54, she won the Vare Trophy for low scoring average, was second on the money list, and was voted the Associated Press Woman Athlete of the Year for the sixth time. Indeed, she was named the A.P. Woman Athlete of the First Half of the 20th Century, and she was probably the best woman athlete of all time.

The only thing Zaharias couldn't beat was cancer. After the first surgery for the malady, she played winning golf into 1955, when she won twice on the Tour. But in June of that year, she was again operated on, and this time she was unable to come back. She died in September 1956 at the age of 42.